MW00849406

"Amy Seiffert's hunger fo
generous compassion are
Name Is Daughter. She's
good friend to every reader who longs to know the God
who loves the unsung women in her book. You will leave
this book more in awe of God, and you will finish it more
aware of your equipping and empowering Father."

Jess Connolly, author of *Tired of Being Tired* and
Breaking Free from Body Shame, host of *The Jess
Connolly Podcast*, founder of Go and Tell Gals, and
pastor at Bright City Church

"Amy has been a good friend of mine for a long time and
is a trusted voice in my life. Her words, which are equal
parts strong, humble, and kind, make questions about
faith and life accessible and relatable. Buckle up; you are
in for a great ride."

Bob Goff, author of the *New York Times* bestsellers *Love
Does*, *Everybody Always*, *Dream Big*, and *Undistracted*

"To be a daughter is to be an heir, and women are heirs to
a powerful legacy. That is the rallying cry of *Your Name
Is Daughter*, which showcases the many boss ladies of
the Bible. With humor, relatability, and a deep knowledge
of Scripture, Amy Seiffert is calling women up! Are you
ready?"

Sharon Hodde Miller, author of *The Cost of Control*

"I devoured this book! Amy shows us a fresh way of seeing
God's heart for women. This book will help you experience some women of the Bible you have never known and
understand some of the assignments God had for women
you may have never noticed. Every woman needs this book
to stand confident in who God designed her to be!"

Jamie Ivey, podcast host and author

"Amy powerfully unpacks our divine identity as beloved
daughters of God with a perspective that pierces the heart

of every woman. With timeless truths that empower us to live boldly in our God-given gifts, this insightful read equips us to embrace life's complexities with faith and confidence. What a refreshing reminder that we were made for this! Our identities are secure, rooted in love and purpose. A must-read!"

Rebekah Lyons, bestselling author of *Rhythms of Renewal* and *Building a Resilient Life*

"Amy Seiffert's *Your Name Is Daughter* is a profound and uplifting exploration of the often overlooked women of the Bible. Seiffert beautifully illustrates how women, though once unseen, are deeply known and cherished by God. This Bible study is a heartfelt reminder to every woman that she is seen and valued and truly belongs. A must-read for anyone seeking inspiration and affirmation of their worth."

Latasha Morrison, author of the *New York Times* bestseller *Be the Bridge*

"This is the book I needed to read ten years ago! Amy gives the reader a full picture of women in the Bible and of how God created them to use their gifts fully in and outside the church. She straddles the line of incredible research in academia and heartfelt stories that make you laugh. Every woman and man needs this on their bookshelf—it will quite possibly change your life. And your church."

Jami Nato, author of *This Must Be the Place*

"Drawing upon solid biblical and theological scholarship, Amy Seiffert exercises a faithful and compelling theological imagination. Faithful to the biblical text and with captivating storytelling skills, she pours healing and hope into the grist and gristle of women's experience. This is how theology should be merged with life."

Dr. Don J. Payne, Denver Seminary, vice president of academic affairs and professor of theology

YOUR
NAME IS
DAUGHTER

Books by Amy Seiffert

Your Name Is Daughter
Your Name Is Daughter Bible Study
Starved
Starved Bible Study
Grace Looks Amazing on You
Chin Up

YOUR NAME IS DAUGHTER

WHAT THE UNSUNG WOMEN OF THE BIBLE TEACH US ABOUT OUR WORTH

AMY SEIFFERT

BETHANYHOUSE

a division of Baker Publishing Group
Minneapolis, Minnesota

© 2025 by Amy Seiffert

Published by Bethany House Publishers
Minneapolis, Minnesota
BethanyHouse.com

Bethany House Publishers is a division of
Baker Publishing Group, Grand Rapids, Michigan

Printed in the United States of America

All rights reserved. No part of this publication may be reproduced, stored in a retrieval system, or transmitted in any form or by any means—for example, electronic, photocopy, recording—without the prior written permission of the publisher. The only exception is brief quotations in printed reviews.

Library of Congress Cataloging-in-Publication Data
Names: Seiffert, Amy, author.
Title: Your name is daughter : what the unsung women of the Bible teach us about our worth / Amy Seiffert.
Description: Minneapolis, Minnesota : Bethany House Publishers, a division of Baker Publishing Group, [2025] | Includes bibliographical references.
Identifiers: LCCN 2024039014 | ISBN 9780764243646 (paperback) | ISBN 9780764244636 (casebound) | ISBN 9781493449675 (ebook)
Subjects: LCSH: Christian women—Religious life. | Christian life—Biblical teaching. | Women in the Bible.
Classification: LCC BV4527 .S345 2025 | DDC 248.8/43—dc23/eng/20240925
LC record available at https://lccn.loc.gov/2024039014

Unless otherwise indicated, Scripture quotations are from THE HOLY BIBLE, NEW INTERNATIONAL VERSION®, NIV® Copyright © 1973, 1978, 1984, 2011 by Biblica, Inc.® Used by permission. All rights reserved worldwide.

Scripture quotations labeled CSB have been taken from the Christian Standard Bible®, copyright © 2017 by Holman Bible Publishers. Used by permission. Christian Standard Bible® and CSB® are federally registered trademarks of Holman Bible Publishers.

Scripture quotations labeled ESV are from The Holy Bible, English Standard Version® (ESV®), copyright © 2001 by Crossway, a publishing ministry of Good News Publishers. Used by permission. All rights reserved. ESV Text Edition: 2016.

Scripture quotations labeled MSG are taken from THE MESSAGE, copyright © 1993, 2002, 2018 by Eugene H. Peterson. Used by permission of NavPress. All rights reserved. Represented by Tyndale House Publishers, Inc.

Scripture quotations labeled NASB are from the New American Standard Bible® (NASB), copyright © 1960, 1962, 1963, 1968, 1971, 1972, 1973, 1975, 1977, 1995 by The Lockman Foundation. Used by permission. www.Lockman.org

Scripture quotations labeled NLT are taken from the Holy Bible, New Living Translation, copyright © 1996, 2004, 2015 by Tyndale House Foundation. Used by permission of Tyndale House Publishers, Carol Stream, Illinois 60188. All rights reserved.

Scripture quotations labeled NLV are taken from the New Life Version, copyright © 1969 and 2003. Used by permission of Barbour Publishing, Inc., Uhrichsville, Ohio 44683. All rights reserved.

Cover design by Micah Kandros Design

Published in association with The Bindery Agency, TheBinderyAgency.com

Baker Publishing Group publications use paper produced from sustainable forestry practices and postconsumer waste whenever possible.

25 26 27 28 29 30 31   7 6 5 4 3 2 1

To my dad.

You mirrored our Heavenly Father all the time.
You never made me question how loved I am
or whose daughter I was.

CONTENTS

INTRODUCTION

Well, you and I don't have to kill ourselves. We are the Beloved. We are intimately loved long before our parents, teachers, spouses, children, and friends loved or wounded us. That's the truth of our lives. That's the truth I want you to claim for yourself. That's the truth spoken by the voice that says, "You are my Beloved."

—Henri Nouwen, *Life of the Beloved*

I had questions.

But I wasn't always sure where to put them, if they were allowed, or if my questions were too weighty, like the last girl stepping into a jam-packed canoe, making the whole thing wobble and sway and eventually tip over. And then everyone would be standing there in the muddy river, sopping wet and looking at an upside-down canoe, sending dagger eyes to the girl who rocked the boat. I didn't want to be that girl.

From the moment I first opened the Bible at sixteen, and started reading all the wild stories of love and betrayal and devotion and pain, I began noticing a pattern. There were so many dudes.

And being the woman that I am, I wondered if this meant women were supposed to be in the background. Were women less important to God? What did the stories and poetry and Gospels tell us about the kingdom of God and how sons and daughters ought to live? What does each woman's story tell us if they are few and far between?

So, this book has been writing itself for thirty years. It's the compilation of scribbled questions inside my coffee-stained, half-finished journals (I'm a fair-weather journaler, at best). It's all the heavily underlined verses that told me about God's heart for His daughters. It's the tears in prayer, asking for things to shift. It's the whispered curiosity from college girls in coffee shop corners, looking at me for answers. It's the search to see if God wanted women to only do certain things. It's the possibility that God's heart for His daughters has been hidden and I had missed it—we had missed it. It's a treasure hunt about what the unsung women of the Bible have to tell us about our worth.

This book is also an invitation. I invite you to grab your nearest shovel, to stand with me shoulder to shoulder, and to dig right next to me. Because there are diamonds in the rough, and there is buried treasure begging to be found. We don't need to be afraid to roll up our sleeves and get dirty. The diamonds are there whether we find them or not. But it's way more fun to play in the dirt than to stand and watch others find the jewels.

Speaking of jewels, there's a story in the Bible where Jesus took a dip in the river, and when he stood up, water dripping down his beard—like oil down an anointed king's face— a voice announced something unmistakable. Ask anyone standing on the eastern side of the Jordan River that overcast afternoon. They'd all tell you the same story. They all heard it. Loud and clear: "This is my beloved Son, with whom I am well pleased" (Matthew 3:17 ESV).

My beloved Son. A Son "chosen and marked" by His Father's love, as *The Message* puts it. A Son loved before He had done one miracle. A Son loved not for His performance, not for His good works, not for His wit and charm, not for pulling out an unbelievable buffet from a sack lunch. A Son loved just because the Father is Love. Full stop.

But here's the kicker: God has spoken this over you, too. Yes, you, wearing that shirt for the third day. With the topknot and sweats, or the heels and suit. You, with your past you'd rather forget. You, who struggles to love who she sees in the mirror. You, who feels unseen. You, who was not the kind of friend you wanted to be last week and are battling shame. You, with your beauty and brokenness and brilliance.

Your name is beloved daughter because you have a good Father who has claimed you as His. The same way the heavens divided, the dove descended, and the voice declared. You are the Father's daughter because He stopped what He was doing, turned around to find you, and looked you right in the eyes and said so, with gusto and delight.

How so?

There's a story in the Bible where a woman has been bleeding. For over a decade. Listen, I am mad if my monthly visitor stays longer than five whole days. And Scripture tells us this had been going on for *years*. No amount of dark chocolate and ice cream could make that length of time manageable. So of course, when she heard about Jesus and how he had been healing people, she ditched the chocolate and headed for the door.

The day the suffering woman came to Jesus was both extraordinary and not. It was the day she reached toward Jesus. That was it. She extended her arm. She literally put out her hand. This was nothing fancy or spectacular or particularly special. Which means this reaching is available to anyone. To you and me. And she opened her heart. Again, nothing fancy. She wanted wholeness and she trusted her gut.

And there, on that dusty street in the noisy crowd on an ordinary day, she was named by Jesus. He called her *Daughter*. For years she had taken care of herself. And Jesus's first order of business? To take care of her daughtership. Which is extraordinary.

She had no father going before her, until that day.

When Jesus named her Daughter, He bestowed upon her every blessing that comes with Him being called Beloved Son. If we are in Christ and He is in us, we also are stamped with this irrevocable, extraordinary label: child of God (see John 1:12).

In calling her a daughter, He gave this suffering woman a family, a seat at the dinner table, a place to call home. He gave her throne-room privileges, every spiritual blessing, a full-access pass to His gentle and humble heart. He gave her all the symbolic rings, robes, and shoes—the way the prodigal son was clothed. He poured His overflowing compassion on her heart and body, the way He saw and cared for helpless sheep without a shepherd. He held her face in His hands and said, "Yes, just look at you! You, my beloved daughter, certainly do bear my image."

This story is yours, is mine. The bleeding woman is us. If Jesus turned to the very least of these and claimed her—the woman on the farthest edge of society who grabbed the edge of His shirt, the one marginalized in every possible way—then He has done it for every daughter in between. What a Father we have in Him.

I wrote this book for those of us who have felt unseen, unnoticed, unwelcome. It is for those who wonder how God feels about them and their season, their life stage, and their gifts. For those who have felt stuck for a host of reasons. For those who need fresh imagery for feminine leadership, coming in all shapes and sizes. For those outside the church who wonder how God feels about women. For those inside the church who feel the words of Tara Beth Leach deeply when she says, "The church in North America has an anemic imagination when it comes to women's roles within the church."[1]

This is for those who want to see the truth that when daughters are called by Jesus, they are set free, they are empowered, and they are commissioned. After all, the kingdom of God turns scars to stories and shame to glory and says our mess is most likely our message.

In each chapter my heart is to bring the women in the Bible to life. So you'll see something a little bit different in many chapters as I use fictionalized details to build on a story. My hope for you is to slide on her sandals and experience what she did. So often we miss the sights and smells of a moment in Scripture—of real women who had real lives—and the context surrounding these women. Though drawing from historical research, I'm filling in the details with my holy imagination and my experience as a woman.

So let's roll up our sleeves and grab our shovels. I will introduce you to the prophets, the grandmas, the midwives, and more. You'll see yourself in these women, and you'll see God's delight in you because He delights in them. Let's dig in.

BELONGING

This section is about belonging. Because belonging is central to who daughters are and what they do. They belong to their Father, the one who calls them daughter. They belong at Sunday dinner, they belong in the King's palace, they belong in their baggy sweats, they belong wherever God sends them. There are two other sections after this: healing and receiving. But for now, belonging. Because our belonging has been in question for quite some time.

1

The Daughter

We Are Named

Daughter, your faith has healed you. Go in peace.

Luke 8:48

There was a season of my life when I didn't want to get out of bed. I had young kids who needed help with, well, everything. And I also had a pinched nerve in my neck. The pain was sharp and constant, and simple daily tasks felt impossible and complicated. When morning came *again* after I had just done a whole twenty-four hours of life the day before, I felt defeated before I started. And I imagine that's how our girl right here felt.

Today was one of those days. The kind where she woke up light-headed, barely making it to the bathroom without holding on to the wall for support. *Just hold on, the spots you're seeing always pass,* she told herself. From there, speaking out loud, she coached herself to find the kitchen table. It didn't matter if she talked to herself. No one else was with her; she had been alone for years.

As she slowly diced cucumbers and sorted through her cheeses, she turned over the idea of trying to get close to the guy she heard was in town. The one who people said was curing rare diseases. She certainly qualified for the rare-disease category. Every doctor she had seen was confused. But there would be crowds. And what if the healing was a hoax? Would it be worth the risk?

A wave of dizziness came on again. She closed her eyes, gripped the table, waited for it to pass. But this wave was followed by something else. Something even stronger. What was this? A wave of bravery? Resolve? Faith? It was something strong. Should she let this wave carry her to the possibility of a man who heals?

A large crowd followed and pressed around Him. And in that moment, she knew she had to try. She had suffered a great deal under the care of many doctors and had spent all she had, yet instead of getting better, she grew worse. She came up behind Him in the crowd and touched His cloak, because she thought, "If I just touch his clothes, I will be healed." Immediately her bleeding stopped, and she felt in her body that she was freed from her suffering.

At once Jesus realized that power had gone out from him. He turned around in the crowd and asked, "Who touched my clothes?"

"You see the people crowding against you," his disciples answered, "and yet you can ask, 'Who touched me?'"

But Jesus kept looking around to see who had done it. Then the woman, knowing what had happened to her, came and fell at his feet and, trembling with fear, told him the whole truth. He said to her, "Daughter, your faith has healed you. Go in peace and be freed from your suffering."

Mark 5:30–34

I think of those with chronic physical pain, their doctors gathering around scans, scratching their heads, making their best educated guesses. I think of those with trauma from childhood, triggered and pressed heavy, when all they wanted was to go to church, but the pastor reminds them of their oppressor. I think of those who feel unseen, unwanted, unloved. I think of the one woman who gets three vibrant paragraphs in the Gospels, who had suffered under the care of many doctors.

And I think of the phrase "but no one could heal her"—that's what Luke, the resident doctor of the Gospels, wrote for us in chapter 8, verse 43. He also recorded this story with his own details. Was he personally familiar with her case? Had his fellow contemporaries brought her issues to him? Had this puzzled him, too? But no one could heal her.

Mark has this detail in chapter 5, verse 26, "She had suffered a great deal under the care of many doctors and had spent all she had, yet instead of getting better she grew worse." She spent all she had. Which included money, yes, but also her mental energy, time, self-worth, hope. She spent it all to try to get well. Yet instead of getting better, she grew worse.

And maybe you've spent it all. You've depleted every resource, you've cried all the tears, you've gotten worse. You've tried to find your bootstraps, but they have long since been torn from the seam. God sees you in your pennilessness, in your pain. His face is turned toward you. She is proof for our weary souls.

Twelve years of a mysterious disease that wouldn't quit, that was with her night and day. Twelve years of pain that began to feel invisible to her friends and family. Twelve years of feeling less than in her community.

Luke 8 is a chapter brimming with beauty for us. I don't want you to miss what Luke was doing when he gave us the details that lead up to the bleeding woman. This chapter that holds space for her begins with a list of women who are traveling with Jesus, funding His mission. Luke, a careful bookkeeper, records every name of each woman with Jesus. This entire chapter is woven with women—mothers, sisters, daughters. Each has her own story, own hurts, own joys, own family, own fears, own faith.

> After this, Jesus traveled about from one town and village to another, proclaiming the good news of the kingdom of God. The Twelve were with him, and also some women who had been cured of evil spirits and diseases: Mary (called Magdalene) from whom seven demons had come out; Joanna the wife of Chuza, the manager of Herod's household; Susanna; and many others. These women were helping to support them out of their own means.
>
> Luke 8:1–3

The women traveling had been cured of spirits and suffering. These women traded a life under a roof for a life under the stars. Perhaps they were willing to risk it because Jesus felt the most like home.

Mary Magdalene, Joanna, Susanna, and many others. How many other women? Three? Ten? Twenty? They followed Jesus, like the rest. They supported Jesus, picking up the tab, spending money for food and tents. They were with Him right there next to the Twelve. Hearing what they heard. Eating what they ate. Listening in as students of the Rabbi. Sharing inside jokes, setting up and tearing down tents, making a life on the road.

Let's not miss this. Richard Bauckham writes, "The principle point is what is said equally of the twelve and of the women; that they were 'with' Jesus as he traveled around proclaiming the good news of the kingdom of God. At this stage of Luke's narrative this is the essence of discipleship . . . : to accompany Jesus and to witness his ministry."[1] These women were Jesus's disciples. They were with Him. I love hearing there were many other women *with* Jesus. Because those women are you, me, us.

It's no secret we want to find ourselves in the stories we read. And for years I was often discouraged (which is a very spiritual way of saying frustrated and bitter) by the lack of women. So whenever I saw a woman in Scripture, I immediately slipped on her sandals and walked around in them for long periods of time. What was she doing? What was she saying? What was she thinking? Why was she crying? What was she eating? What does God think of her? When I saw a woman, I saw myself in some way. And because less than 10 percent of the names in the Bible are names of women, this made me want to pay attention to every woman I saw. I wanted to dig up this diamond and see what I had. Because, yes, the backdrop to the Bible is patriarchy, but that was not the blueprint.[2] Jesus never played the patriarchy game. In fact, He worked to dismantle it.

I became fascinated with how Jesus healed and restored women, touched unclean women and made them clean instead of becoming unclean Himself, invited women to learn when the culture wouldn't allow a woman to learn Torah or to recite daily prayers, showcased women in His teaching as examples of faith, and commissioned women to be His disciples. He did this because His Father had done this. God had blessed and empowered both men and women, side by side, to co-rule in the garden of Eden. It's no coincidence that the way of Jesus looks a lot like the garden of Eden. Stay tuned, there's more on this later.

After Luke names the women who were with Jesus, he records Jesus's parable of the sower and the seeds. The disciples ask Jesus to explain what He means by it all because sometimes Jesus talks in riddles. Jesus explains that the "seed is the word of God" (Luke 8:11). Some seeds don't take root. Some do, but they are choked by worries, riches, and pleasures. And then He says, "But the seed on good soil stands for those with a noble and good heart, who hear the word, retain it, and by persevering produce a crop" (Luke 8:15).

Seeds and soil. Hearts and hopes. Crops and crowds. Jesus is bringing the rule and reign of God through stories so that some would hear and understand.

After this story, His own mother and brothers came to see Him, but the crowd—swollen with people—boxed them out. Word reaches Jesus that His family is there. But His response? He says His mother and brothers "are those who hear God's word and put it into practice." His family are those who take God's seed and plant it in good soil. Who travel by faith. Who till the soil of their heart.

Because of the first-century Jewish culture where your family was everything, some scholars have said that this was offensive and a hard saying. But could He possibly be redefining what family is, specifically the family of God? Was Jesus remembering Abraham's family and the call to bless all other nations? N. T. Wright says it this way:

> Jesus was proposing to treat his followers as a surrogate family. This had a substantial positive result: Jesus intended his followers to inherit all the closeness and mutual obligations that belonged with family membership in that close-knit, family-based society.[3]

In creating a surrogate family, it seems Jesus was throwing His arms open wide and gathering more family along the way. More mothers, more sisters, more daughters. More fathers, more brothers, more sons. Come in, come in, come in! You are invited! You can belong! Because the kingdom of God is expansive, wide open, available to anyone who will soften the soil of their heart and follow along.

As Luke writes on, more faith talk ensues as Jesus, asleep in a boat, wakes up to a raging storm. He stands up, tells the waves to sit down, and then asks His disciples where their faith is.

"At the bottom of the lake," one may have whispered.

After a few other twists and turns, they come upon a prominent synagogue leader. He was a very well-known religious leader—like a famous pastor with a large platform, many books, and a soaring Instagram following. He's a big deal. His name was Jairus, and his only girl—his precious twelve-year-old daughter—was terribly sick. She was dying. So he came for Jesus. Because the gift of desperation will do that—make you find Jesus with every emotional penny you have.

Jairus and Jesus set off, surrounded by crowds almost crushing them as they went.

But the crowd carried a woman inside of it, the way a wave carries minnows to shore. A nameless, sick, suffering, marginalized, impoverished woman. With a small seed of faith buried in tender soil, she somehow believed if she could only just touch Jesus's cloak, then she would find the hem of healing.

It's amazing when we think we truly have tried it all, spent it all, prayed it all that somehow, somewhere, we then dig deep to find one more ounce to give. When we don't think we can keep going. When we don't care anymore. When we toss and turn in our bed all night because anxiety is our pillow and fear is our sheets. But there, in the dark, we find a tiny seed is still hidden, still fighting to grow. There is still a buried chance.

And by grace, this seed has fallen on some good soil in our heart—the soil that will produce a crop of faith. Even as tiny as this patch of soil is inside of us.

Since the day Jairus's daughter was born, this woman had been bleeding. It was time for something new to happen at this twelve-year mark. The way twelve new disciples were chosen as the echo of the twelve tribes of Israel. The way a high priest wore a breastplate of authority containing twelve shiny jewels. The way the new Jerusalem has twelve gates, twelve angels, and twelve foundations. Twelve has long been a significant number in the Bible, representing God's "power and authority," God's rule and reign.[4]

And here, with these two women, Jesus ushers in a fresh start for each one. The rule and reign of King Jesus will bring royal healing to the least of these. The rule and reign of King Jesus will turn around and call a nameless woman "Daughter." The rule and reign of King Jesus will know when the last thread of faith reaches for the last thread of His cloak.

Jesus paused His mission with a prominent leader to name an unnamed woman "Daughter." She was worth stopping for. She was worth seeing. She was worth naming.

"Daughter, your faith has healed you. Go in peace" (Luke 8:48). This blessing by Jesus is everything. Each part of the phrase packs a punch.

Daughter.

It should be noted that she's the only one Jesus calls Daughter. The one who snuck through the crowd; long-suffering was her song. The one who had long since been marginalized because blood was unclean. This one He called Daughter was the least likely to attract a king's attention. But He turned around for her on an errand to heal an official's daughter. Because she slid through the crowd with a seed in her heart.

Jairus was a father seeking Jesus on behalf of his daughter. But the woman with an issue of blood had no father advocating for her. We know the other girl because she's somebody's daughter. Jarius's daughter. But this woman has no father in front of her. Alone, she reaches out anyway.

Your faith has healed you.

The mysterious nature of a seed of faith is that we don't know how fast it will grow or what crop it will yield or when it will bloom. There is a flower in the hills of South India that only blooms every twelve years. They are the Neelakurinji flowers, and every twelve years the Kurinji flowers bloom and paint the hills a purplish blue.[5] The majestic hills remind us that there is hope for those who wait and for those who are tired of waiting. For those who reach out and for those who are tired of reaching out. For those who suffer and for those who are tired of suffering.

In your suffering, you are seen. In your suffering, you are called Daughter. In your suffering, you are precious. In your suffering, you are His.

Go in peace.

Peace means wholeness. Shalom. Where things that were divided and torn apart are now bound back together. For the first time in years, she was made whole. In a way she had never known before. At first glance, you might just see her physical healing and wholeness. But I imagine, after years of suffering alone, the greatest sense of peace she felt was the fact that she had been claimed and called. Her name was now Daughter.

But after Jesus stopped and sought out His Daughter, the unthinkable happened. Someone told Jarius it was too late. His daughter had died. James R. Edwards writes, "The interruption, so profitable to the woman, has cost the life of Jairus's daughter."[6]

How dare He.

How dare Jesus prioritize the nameless for the named.

How dare Jesus pause His plans for the prominent to heal the poor.

How dare Jesus search out the hidden gems in our world and name them.

Oh but praise the God who dares!

When Jesus paused His plans for His daughter, all was not lost. There was more to be found. Jesus wanted us all to see the extraordinary faith of the bleeding woman. Her faith was meant to encourage Jarius. And to encourage you and me.

When Jesus heard that Jairus's daughter had died, He said, "Don't be afraid; just believe" (Luke 8:50). Which is exactly what the bleeding woman had just done. In the face of her fear, she believed. Jesus just held up a nameless woman as an example of faith to all of us.

Two women, bound by sickness, by twelve years, by the healing of Jesus. Reminding us to keep a kernel of faith in some soft soil in the deep recesses of our souls. Telling us to reserve the tiniest seed of hope when the night is dark and when "but no one could heal her" is our song. Painting the image of Jesus turning around, feeling healing power leave Him, for when we need to know daughters are called.

In your suffering, you are seen. Your seed of faith matters. Your name is Daughter.

2

The Ezer

We Have Always Belonged

Blessed are you, Israel! Who is like you, a people saved by the LORD? He is your shield and *helper* and your glorious sword.

Deuteronomy 33:29 (emphasis added)

We started with a sick, obscure, unnamed woman who reached out to Jesus. And then Jesus reached right back, meeting one of the deepest needs she had, calling her Daughter. But let's back up. All the way up. To where the earth was just beginning. Because I don't want you to miss how our worth as daughters is woven into the very fabric of creation.

When the world was being made, you could hear it. You could hear joy. Joy boomed from God's voice in this work of creation. Brimming with anticipation—smiling ear to ear—God lassoed chaos with his tongue, hog-tied disorder with his orders. He announced life, harmony, shalom. And soon enough, the garden was teeming with *tov*, the Hebrew word for *good*, "the idea of being in harmony with God,"[1] everything dancing with delight to the song of our hearts. All was in sync, in rhythm to a cosmic beat.

As light pierced through darkness for the very first time, God declared it good. Illuminating what is true, what is real, what is hidden. The way your fingers desperately slide along the wall, finally catching the switch in the hall at 2:00 a.m. and you are led to your crying baby's crib. The way the story of abuse tumbles out of your friend's mouth and your heart shifts—and really sees and grasps and understands why she has lived with deep anxiety and trauma for years. The way a lazy summer afternoon fades into night, but the faint glow from the fireflies tells you where your peonies are planted. Light has been born, and it is good.

Then more goodness inside of goodness. The Master Gardener playfully slid seeds inside of plants, like little wombs ready to bring life. The way the Father and Son and Holy Spirit unexpectedly hid life inside of death, tucked tov inside of tombs. The mysteries never cease, from the beginning until now.

Then every kind of animal started breathing, swimming, flying. Every little hummingbird leaving a trail of joy, freedom, and perseverance. Each creature good, gardened by a good God. The land and sea ones, and the ones that can somehow mysteriously live in both. The adaptable amphibians, breathing oxygen and absorbing water through thin skin. All shades and shapes. Including the wild Pumpkin Toadlets, who gloriously glow in the dark.

It is good and good and good. Harmony, harmony, harmony.

But then, it's not.

What was that? It's not good? What's not good?

It is not good for man to be alone.

Like a scrape across a record's song. The musical dissonance? So obvious. This was not sin, but this was out of sync. No animal was suitable to co-reign with Adam. Adam had named them all, but still, he was lacking. God knew what was missing, showed Adam what was missing, and He wanted us to see it, too. And the drama takes a turn. All was in harmony with God. Until it was not.

Something good was missing. Something good must still be made. Something good was needed. The way armor without a shield leaves someone unprotected. And a warrior without a sword is defenseless. And battle without strength is hopeless.

So an *ezer* was crafted. A woman. A daughter of God.

What's this about shields and swords and strength? Haven't we, so often, heard about sidekicks and second-class citizens and silence?

Ezer

Eve is created and called *ezer* in Hebrew. Ezer is translated as *helper*, and that's how it is typically expressed in many churches. Eve was made to be a helper. And while this is a true definition, the word has a richer, fuller meaning. It's a word full of strength and shield, protection and power. And despite what you may have heard in Bible study, it's a word not only about women. It's a word about God.

Sixteen out of the twenty-one times ezer was used in the Old Testament refer to Yahweh Himself.[2] A mighty Help in battle, a Defender from enemies, a Shield for armor. The Bible Project calls Eve a "delivering ally."[3] And as Shara Drimalla points out:

> Then God calls this woman an "*ezer kenegdo*." The Hebrew word *ezer* might be translated as "help," but it does not

mean what we often assume. An *'ezer* is not a lesser "assistant" or "helper" as much as it is someone who plays a mutual role of "the indispensable other," a strong and wise guide, without whom the intended good cannot happen. The only other character in the Bible given this title (*'ezer*) is God himself. Not your average helper, right?

For the second Hebrew word, *kenegdo*, we might use a metaphor of mirroring to get to the core idea. A helpful paraphrase of Genesis 2:18 might be: "It is not good for the human to be solitary. I will make one who can deliver him from his inability to fulfill the divine commission alone, one who mirrors him."[4]

The woman God crafted is fully equal, fully image-bearing, fully blessed by God.

Sometimes I like to think of Eve as a lifeguard. *Eve* means life, and she is well suited to guard it. But may we have the imagination to replace the idea of a bored and sunburned teenager, swinging her whistle around her finger to the beat of the Top 40 Hits, with that of an attentive and compassionate guardian, walking and surveying the waters, bringing safety and security to her environment. She is the keeper of life, she is ready to defend, she is strong and equipped for the job.

In almost every situation we see God described as ezer, it is a life-and-death situation. A great rescue is needed, a strong intervention. There are twenty-one places in the Bible God calls Himself our helper, our ezer. Here are a few:

> There is no one like the God of Jeshurun, who rides across the heavens to *help* you . . . Blessed are you, Israel! Who is like you, a people saved by the LORD? He is your shield and *helper* and your glorious sword.
>
> Deuteronomy 33:26, 29, emphasis added

I lift up my eyes to the mountains—where does my *help* come from? My *help* comes from the LORD, the Maker of heaven and earth.

> Psalm 121:1–2, emphasis added

May the LORD answer you when you are in distress; may the name of the God of Jacob protect you. May he send you *help* . . .

> Psalm 20:1–2, emphasis added

We wait in hope for the LORD; he is our *help* and our shield.

> Psalm 33:20, emphasis added

All you Israelites, trust in the LORD—he is their *help* and shield. House of Aaron, trust in the LORD—he is their *help* and shield. You who fear him, trust in the LORD—he is their *help* and shield.

> Psalm 115:9–11, emphasis added

Yes, ezer is translated as helper. But we must recover the goodness that was gardened the day a great help arrived. Eve was not relegated to the kitchen of Eden; she wasn't told to make dinner and stay behind the scenes. She was given a co-equal, co-reigning, co-working job. Eve was made in the image of the "delivering ally"[5] of God.

Imago Dei

But, some may ask, was being created second somehow second-class? Not when the creation story clearly states,

> So God created mankind in his own image,
>   in the image of God he created them;
>   male and female he created them.

God blessed them and said to them, "Be fruitful and increase in number; fill the earth and subdue it. Rule over the fish in the sea and the birds in the sky and over every living creature that moves on the ground."

Genesis 1:27–28

From the beginning—at the very start of it all—the plan was for both of us to belong, all along. Side by side. Eve wasn't an afterthought. She wasn't Plan B.

The words *image of God* in Latin are *imago Dei*. The image, the picture, the representation of God. Male and female, they image God. Male and female, they were blessed. Male and female, they were commissioned to be fruitful, increase, fill the earth, rule over it. Together. Before they were both cursed, they were both blessed. Glenn Kreider writes:

> No idea of superiority/inferiority with respect to the sexes can be found here. That woman was taken from man no more implies the inferiority of woman to man than the taking of man from the ground . . . implies the inferiority of man to the ground.[6]

In light of this, let's not ever forget that the first imprint upon humanity was blessing. A blessing upon both male and female to cultivate the goodness of the earth. To co-rule, co-create, co-image God. And this holy imprint still remains. We continue to uncover this holy imprint—to be transformed into the good and very good—that had its beginning in the garden, where, side by side, men and women cultivate the earth and create and reflect goodness in the image of their Creator.

The blessing didn't include a hierarchy, and the subduing was never of one human over another. The blessing commissioned humans to rule the earth together; the curse described humans ruling over one another. The blessing was for both man and woman to live in harmony. The dissonance came after. As Scot McKnight writes:

> Sadly, some think Genesis 3:16 is a *prescription* for the relationship of women and men for all time. Instead of a prescription, these two lines are a *prediction* of the fallen desire of fallen women and fallen men in a fallen condition in a fallen world. Fallen women yearn to dominate men, and fallen men yearn to dominate women. The desire to dominate is a broken desire. The redeemed desire is to love in mutuality. This verse in Genesis 3, in other words, predicts a struggle of fallen wills; they don't prescribe how we are *supposed* to live.[7]

Much later, as the curse wove its way through history, we find it in first-century kitchens. Martha bravely brought her full self, her frustrations, her feelings to Jesus. She asked Jesus to tell Mary to help her with the meal-making instead of joining His disciples, learning as one of them, at His feet. Jesus and His apprentices had come to stay and dinner was cooking and the list of things to do was long.

But Jesus's response? It's as if He said, *My daughters are free to learn. There is a time for cooking and a time for learning at my feet. She has chosen a good thing. She chose tov, just as it was in the beginning. She is sitting at my feet, just like my disciples, learning and listening to a new way of life. A life that frees the oppressed, liberates the captives. A life that invites Gentiles and sinners, Canaanites and cancerous, the left-outs and the sell-outs, the prostitutes and the prominent to my table. A life where neither kitchens nor classrooms are gendered. Where I declare every ezer Daughter. Where I declare every unloved one Loved. Where I declare every second-class citizen first-class. Where I declare the societally invisible Image-bearers.*

Tsela

The making of a daughter, an ezer, all happened when Adam was asleep. Sometimes the goodness of God makes us lie down in green pastures and wakes us up with surprise and delight. One of Adam's ribs was fashioned into an ezer. But maybe we need to wake up to a fuller picture of a small bone in his side? Was it just a rib? Or was something much bigger at play?

Rib is the word *tsela* in Hebrew. And why all this talk about the original Hebrew? Stay with me—the beauty is worth the translation aerobics. While this has famously been translated as *rib*, it is actually more of a whole side. Preston Sprinkle disagrees with the translation here, "since *tsela* occurs more than forty other times in the Old Testament and it *never means 'rib.'*" In almost every other usage, *tsela* refers to the side of a sacred piece of architecture. . . ."[8] Shara Drimalla and the BibleProject Team expand on this idea:

> The biblical authors use *tsela* to refer to the two halves of the ark of the covenant, the two halves of the temple, and the two halves of the new Jerusalem. So God's creation of Eve is a process of dividing Adam in half and then building Eve from one side of him. We get a portrait of two humans, each one half of a united whole, deeply dependent on the other. Adam's goodness and life depends on Eve, and hers depends on his.[9]

A whole side. A side of a building, an ark, a hill, a temple. The way the temple was filled with God's glory and later our bodies were named the temple of the Spirit of God. The half of Adam was used to make Eve. And if humanity was missing an entire half of the whole image of God? That certainly wasn't good. Adam wasn't missing someone who would just help him achieve his dreams and support his job. Humanity itself was missing a whole half of the image of God, one who mirrored Adam, who would be both strength and shield.

Stories matter. And how we pass a story on, how we paint the picture, how we see the first image-bearers matters. Because we know stories do at least two things (and of course one million more). Stories create emotional connection for us, and stories preserve a culture. For instance, there's a story about my great-grandmother who was a stowaway at twelve years old. She boarded a ship to the United States in 1915 right before WWI hit her country of Czechoslovakia. Knowing this story and retelling this story preserves the memory of my grandmother's grit and the culture of my own family. Or, much less heroically, the story when my uncle, one Christmas Eve at midnight mass, took communion and then whispered, "Thanks, Jesus. You're delicious." And this irreverently funny comment was passed down the pew to each adult family member, one by one, telephone-game style. And as the clock struck midnight and the majesty of our Savior's birth was upon us, so was the subtle shaking of a pew from my family's muffled laughter. We retell this story around Christmas, preserving my family's culture of faith with a side of irreverence.

The culture of the kingdom of God has often included a story about "a suitable helper" in the garden, leaving us with a malnourished picture of what God built. What if we told the story using the words *ezer* and *imago Dei* and *tsela*? What if we made sure our daughters knew God pictured Himself when He made His daughters? A mighty help in war, in crisis, in life-and-death situations? What if helping wasn't about being in the background but about occupying a rightful side-by-side nature in the foreground? What if we are both called, sons and daughters, to display the glory of God side by side? What if daughters are called to every kind of helping imaginable?

We would have a riveting story, indeed.

I see daughters all around me whose own stories tell the story of God—these are daughters just like you. I see you, as you help prepare meals and help prepare hearts, as you help fight for justice and help a fevered infant in the night. You help create carpooling charts like nobody's business and create new government policies so the marginalized have access to the care they need. You help through tears and with tenacity. You help rescue and help restore. You help the harassed and help the harasser. You help at home and help in the marketplace. You help with prayer and with power. You help silently and you help loudly. You help with lament and with leadership. You help while afraid and help while bold. You help by faith and you help in doubt. You help with joy and you help with sadness. You help with clean hands and you help with dirty ones. You help with mixed motives and you help with clear eyes. You help begrudgingly and you help beautifully. You help in different ways at different seasons at different times in your lives. And with each act of helping—of rescuing—you bear God's image.

And as we help, we not only tell the story of God's creation, but we show it. We are an intentional part of the creation story, where every creature was named and yet still Adam lacked. Our bodies were fashioned like gorgeous pieces of architecture, mirroring Adam's glorious body, temples that would later house God Himself, starting with Mary the mother of God and leading up to us right now, temples where the Spirit of God dwells at all times.

Adam woke up completely delighted, by the way. Joy was restored, harmony was back. With an ezer in the garden, the song was soothing again. And Adam sang in joy. An entire side was taken from Adam, indicating the side-by-side nature of their reign. The mirror image of him, fully equipped to cultivate the garden.

And it was very good.

I once found myself in a room full of church leaders and pastors. They were all men. And then there was me. One of these things was not like the others. We had come from all over the country to talk ministry strategies. As I was in line for the taco bar for dinner that evening, a kind, curious guy asked me a question I'll never forget: "So, how did you get here?"

He didn't mean by what vehicle—car or plane or bus. He meant how did I, a woman, get into a room filled with male ministry leaders. Unsure how to answer him, I stumbled over some dumb response as I added jalapeños I didn't want on my tacos.

The answer was that I arrived in the room by a warm invitation from my lead pastor. I was on his staff team as the Director of Outward Movement. That's how I got there. An act of invitation, welcome, and belief in me.

To be sure, hardly ever is any white male asked how they arrived in any location, social or physical. They just walk in, no questions asked. Which is privilege. But us daughters—every color, size, and shape—have felt and fielded the question for years. Whether it was directly asked or indirectly felt. The question of belonging lurks around the edges of boardrooms, of churches, of hospitals, of film crews, of seminaries, of football fields, of universities, of almost any possible place one could think of.

So this book honors the daughters of old, daughters who have gone before us, who felt unseen and unnamed. The daughters we see God speak to and speak through, the daughters who are named and unnamed in the story, the daughters who defended justice and righteousness, the daughters who prophesied and led men into battle, who shouted with joy with fellow pregnant cousins, who changed the course of history for God's people.

And this book is for the daughters of now. Mine and yours. You and me. Your sisters and mothers, your aunts and cousins. The daughters God has called, has equipped, has placed His Spirit—not a lesser spirit but the powerful, authoritative Spirit of God—inside of to commune with and enjoy and hear Him.

And this book is for the daughters who might need reminding that they do, in fact, belong in the room. At the table. The way a woman walked into an important dinner party and knelt before Jesus, weeping and wiping His feet with her tears, her perfume, her hair—using her entire body to anoint Jesus in a room full of men. And Jesus fully welcomed her in, saw her, blessed her, defended her, loved her, and honored her.

3

The Obscure

We Are Seen

The king of Egypt said to the Hebrew midwives, whose names
were Shiphrah and Puah, "When you are helping the Hebrew
women during childbirth on the delivery stool, if you see that
the baby is a boy, kill him; but if it is a girl, let her live." The
midwives, however, feared God and did not do what the king
of Egypt had told them to do; they let the boys live.

Exodus 1:15–17

There are five women I simply adore. I'm talking fangirl
status. If you and I walked into a party together and I saw
them snacking on cheese and drinking cocktails, I would
low-key squeal, grab your arm, and tell you I must introduce
you to these gals. Because they are responsible for changing
the course of history. But they're an unlikely group: two
midwives, a young mom, a teenager, and a princess . . . walk
into a bar. Just kidding. But it's no joke what they pulled off.

"He's asking for us again, Shiphrah. What are we going to say? We've let so many of them live."

Puah, looking at Shiphrah, fidgeted with her hands like she did when she was anxious. Which wasn't often. On a daily basis, her hands were steady, sure, seasoned. A midwife by trade, she had coached countless mothers in distress through the frightening pain of giving birth. Her triumphant hands held the trembling hands of mothers who were staring down death in the face of new life. Her hands were created to bring life into the world. Even though every birth reminded her of her own empty arms.

Puah and Shiphrah had been midwifing together for what seemed like decades. They always shared new tricks of the trade, different herbs and spices that helped with the process, what positions to try to help the mother stay comfortable, what to try to turn a baby around the right way.

But neither midwife had her own children. They had welcomed countless gifts into the world, into the arms of new mothers, fulfilling the greatest honor their culture knew for women to have. Some days their own empty wombs were the only thing on their minds; other days they were so absorbed in their work they didn't think of themselves at all. Going tirelessly from mother to mother, they were some of the best compassionate caretakers in all of Egypt. So said many of their patients.

And the biggest driving force in their life? Their faith in the Giver of Life. The Creator God was their Strength, their Provider, their Hope. They reverently worshiped God.

When the king of Egypt, Pharaoh himself, had summoned them the first time, he'd asked them to do the unthinkable.

His orders were loud and clear. And so was his insecurity. "When you help the Hebrew women give birth, kill the Hebrew boys. They will grow up and increase in number and could band against me and my kingdom and make an army too large to control. So it's your job to snuff them out. Get to it. You can let the girls live for all I care."

They left, tears tumbling down their brown and beautiful faces.

The choice before them? Kill or be killed. What in the world? What had this government come to? What level of power-hungry, fear-based monstrosity had the king arrived at?

What were they going to do?

But just as soon as they left the palace, they got word of being needed by a Hebrew mother. No sooner than they arrived, she was bearing down, and a beautiful, helpless, magnificent baby boy had taken his first breath. Puah and Shiphrah glanced at one another, nodded the slightest nod of solemn agreement—an unspoken pact as bringers of life—and handed the boy right to his mother.

In that moment their eyes said it all: *We will bring life. We are ezers. We are lifeguards. We are rescuers and defenders. We are daughters made in the image of God. The first mother, Eve, meant "life," and we will honor her lineage. Above all, we will honor the Alpha and Omega, the beginning and the end of all breath.*

As the months went on, with each baby born at the hands of Shiphrah and Puah, they risked their lives to bring more life. And then Pharaoh caught wind of it and called them back again to speak with them.

So the king of Egypt called for the midwives. "Why have you done this?" he demanded. "Why have you allowed the boys to live?"

"The Hebrew women are not like the Egyptian women," the midwives replied. "They are more vigorous and have their babies so quickly that we cannot get there in time."

So God was good to the midwives, and the Israelites continued to multiply, growing more and more powerful. And because the midwives feared God, he gave them families of their own.

Exodus 1:18–21 NLT

We must pause here at the story and let the words linger: "God was good to the midwives . . ." and He "gave them families of their own" (vv. 20–21 NLT).

How many babies had Shiphrah and Puah held, longing to fill their arms with their own? And God had seen them. He had heard their cry—like a nursing mother who hears the needs and desires of her infant—and responded with a deep, guttural, moving empathy.

"God was good to the midwives"—something Paul later echoed in his letter to the Philippians as he wrote, "[H]e who began a good work in you will bring it to completion . . ." (Philippians 1:6 ESV). God is good—very much like the goodness of the garden in Genesis—to the midwives. He brought them good, and He was delighted to do so. And somehow their faith played a part in God's gift. The mysterious cocktail of faith and God's blessing was at work in these women. But we know this is not an if-then formula (if we honor God, then He will give us what we want); it's just part of their story. And it is good.

Shiphrah and Puah are the first of five women in the narrative to bring Moses into the story of God's people. These are the obscure ones, easily passed over to get to the parting of the seas and the fiery mountain and the chiseled stone commands. But before any glitz and glam, there was gritty faith. They were the courageous forerunners, going against the king's orders, to honor the one true King. And because of them? The Hebrew nation multiplied. God's people expanded, and so did God's kingdom.

If you feel in the background, Shiphrah and Puah are for you. If you have been shoved between a rock and a hard place? These daughters have gone before you. If you are working quietly behind the scenes to bring life in dark places with words of encouragement, prayers whispered in the dark, strategies to change mindsets, or justice where there is none?

You are seen. If you feel exhausted by doing the right thing? Your Father is proud of you, daughter. May you be seen and honored as they were. What these midwives did matters, and what you do matters, too. Take courage.

After these two courageous midwives, three more women show up in the story and change the course of history. Enter Jochebed, the mother of Moses; Miriam, Jochebed's first-born daughter; and Pharaoh's daughter—the princess—notorious yet nameless in the text.

So you've met Shiphrah and Puah. Next, here's our girl Jochebed (see Exodus 2:1–10).

Her muscular thighs cradled the basket—shaped like a tiny ark—between her knees. Tar was drying on the inside, and soon she'd apply pitch to the outside as a waterproofing agent. *How many coats?* she wondered. *Three? Four?* It's not like she'd done this before, preparing a floating cradle to hold one of her children. Miriam and Aaron were free to live, breathe, toddle, play, and be seen by any Egyptian who happened to come by. But her sweet, youngest, cooing baby boy? He wasn't so lucky. He had to be hidden; the older two had to swear he wasn't there. Even though she was a pro by her third baby, her anxiety was highest with this one. With every cry, she jumped. She anxiously rushed to soothe him so that no one could tell that this baby cry was one of a beautiful baby *boy*.

A boy.

Puah, her beloved midwife, had whispered the news to her when he came out right before the woman handed him to Jochebed. And she couldn't hold back her own cry. His was a cry gulping in life; hers was a cry choking back death.

How long, O Lord? How long must your people suffocate under the hand of the oppressor? How long must this racism endure? How long, O Lord, until you rescue your people from slavery?

She had no idea she held God's provision in her arms.

Jochebed shows us that when we face an impossible situation, God is so close. He is so present. He is working in your waiting. Maybe you are facing a situation you aren't sure how to navigate, but you are taking the next step by faith. Maybe you feel brave about it, or maybe your knees buckle at the thought. May Jochebed encourage you. She took steps in the face of oppression, in the face of uncertainty, in the face of fear. She made a tiny ark to carry her precious cargo. And she did it by faith. Because there's no other way to ship your son down the river if not by trusting God to cradle him while you can't. She thought about her child, stressing about the future, trying her best to trust God. Somehow she fought to remember that God is in control. God took care of her details. And He will take care of yours.

And now for the courageous Miriam.

She had just changed her brother Aaron's diaper and was about to ask her mother what vegetables to chop for dinner when Jochebed came around the corner in the kitchen, worry in her eyes.

"It's not the kitchen where I'll need your help today, Miriam. It's by the river."

Jochebed carefully laid out her plans to her oldest. Her daughter, her strong helper, her little ezer. Growing up as a woman right before her eyes. Her heart swelling with pride, she shared her plan with Miriam. She would put her baby brother in the reeds of the river so that the basket would barely move, so that somehow God would compassionately work on her behalf. She knew this particular spot to be one where women came to bathe. Could they possibly have pity on a baby boy? She prayed like she had never prayed before.

And Miriam's job? Stand by, hidden, to watch and wait. Her mother had counted on her to be responsible and timely all her life, and this moment was no different. Or, rather, this moment was quite possibly the most significant moment of being the oldest she had ever known. Her mother carefully explained how she was overwhelmed with grief at the thought of putting him in the river and that she would have to walk away. But Miriam must stay and intervene if the time was right. *Look for your opportunity. Trust the God of Jacob. He goes before you.*

No pressure, thought Miriam, her snarky thoughts alive and well.

Miriam shows us what it looks like to be tasked with a job too big to handle. If insecurity is rising about something you have to do, Miriam says you are not alone. She didn't know how either, but she did the best she could with what she had.

Friend, God isn't looking for flawless, He's looking for faithful.

And finally, the princess.

They set out to the river to cool down and bathe at their regular spot. The princess and her maids laughed easily and talked among themselves about the latest fashion, the loveliest fabrics, the cutest Egyptian boys. It was another beautiful afternoon, the reeds of the Nile swaying in the wind. The frogs sang a sleepy tune. But underneath the girl talk, the princess had heavier thoughts than most girls. She had grown up in the palace, where she heard heated discussions, political strategies, and racial slurs against the Hebrews. She never said anything out loud, but she continued to grow uncomfortable with how the Hebrews were treated around her. And the decree to kill every male baby? If the princess dwelled too long on it, her stomach turned. Deciding it was best to stick to the latest gossip, the princess buried her thoughts and smiled again at the girls.

As she enjoyed the cool water, her thoughts began to wander again. And so did her eyes. Sweeping the landscape, her gaze stopped on an intricately woven . . . basket? Was that what it was? Bobbing up and down in a cluster of thick reeds?

"Girls, do you see that? What's that caught in the reeds over there?" She asked a maid to take a closer look.

Parting the reeds the way a mother parts her daughter's hair, her maid revealed a floating basket, carefully crafted and beautifully tarred. She loosened the basket from the grasses and floated it toward the princess.

But then they heard it. *Was that a cry? Like a baby? Where was it coming from? Surely not . . . the basket!?*

Her attendant opened the basket, and the cry went from muffled to full-throttled wail. As soon as Pharaoh's daughter saw the baby, compassion filled her body, empathy pulsed through her veins. Instantly remembering the horrible orders from her father that all Hebrew boys must be thrown into the Nile, she marveled at the ingenuity of the mother of this baby. She followed orders all right. But no one had said anything against making an ark when throwing him into the river. Admirable, resourceful, smart. These Hebrew women weren't animals; they were women, like she was. They were humans, like she was. They were intelligent, like she was. And enough was enough, if she had anything to do with it.

"This must be one of the Hebrew babies," the princess breathed.

Miriam stayed alert. She had watched Pharaoh's daughter walk by and descend into the water, chattering and splashing playfully.

She had one eye on the basket holding her family's most precious cargo, one eye on the princess.

Can you imagine having women just attend to you all day, make sure you have everything you need, carry shade plants over your head, answer your every beck and call? She dreamed. *I would order raisin cakes dripping with honey all day long!*

A tiny cry interrupted her daydream. She knew that cry anywhere. And then the women opened the basket, and her baby brother's lungs let loose. Poor thing—how terrible to be stuck in a basket in the river, wondering where his momma was. Speaking of her mother, she wanted to make her proud. And now was her moment.

"Excuse me! Um, hi. I was just passing by, here, in the ummm . . . bushes . . . and I wondered if you wanted me to go and get one of the Hebrew women to nurse this adorable little one for you?"

Pharaoh's daughter clearly had no idea where Miriam had come from, but—yes!—she could see this baby was obviously hungry and welcomed her help.

Miriam's legs had never run faster. Colliding into one another, breathless Miriam and tear-stained Jochebed talked over each other.

"The princess!" "Pharaoh's daughter!" "She wants you to come . . ." "They found our baby boy . . ." "She had pity on him. Come at once!"

Miriam had only heard stories of her mother's speed and epic foot races against all the boys when she was young. Today she experienced it. So that's where Miriam got it. But before she took off with gold-medal speed, Jochebed made quick instructions to their neighbor to please take care of her three-year-old Aaron and then was out of sight before her neighbor could holler *challah*.

Jochebed, getting nearer with every step, could hear her baby's desperate cries, and her body responded. Her milk was letting down as she turned the corner and stopped in her tracks.

Pharaoh's daughter—royal, powerful, beautiful—was holding her son.

She almost fainted, her mind buzzing a mile a minute.

He is in the arms of our oppressor! He is safe from the river . . . but he is in danger! What was she thinking? Why did she think it was a good idea to put him in harm's way? But there was pity in the princess's eyes, just as she had hoped. *Thank God! But now what? Please just give me my son back! I hadn't mentally prepared to see the daughter of the evil man who demanded my son die in the river now holding my baby.*

"Hello there," Pharaoh's daughter said to Jochebed. "We just found this Hebrew baby in the water. And as I pulled him out, I called him Moses. Isn't that an adorable name? Please take him home with you; that nice girl said she knew someone who could nurse him. I shall pay you to take care of him. But since I did, indeed, find him, when he is weaned, bring him back to me, and I will raise him here. He will be the most finely educated boy, learning from only the best Egyptians in the land. He seems to almost glow, this little one. I think your God has big plans for him."

And just like that, Moses was back in his mother's arms. Glory!

Later that evening, Amram and Jochebed passed around baby Moses as every single detail was recounted along with tears and doting and kissing. Miriam took center stage and recalled every expression of each attendant, describing every detail of the day, imitating their every move, reveling in her job well done. They kissed Moses, smothered him with squeezes, laughed, cried, repeat. Had life ever been sweeter? Had their God ever been kinder? What goodness and blessing to have him back! They sang, worshiped, and let the night fall on their good fortune. And baby Moses had no clue what had just transpired. How he was set in the river, intercepted by the oppressor's daughter, returned to his mother's arms. All in a day's work.

Jochebed nursed and rocked her boy to sleep, like she had done for the past three months. God was so faithful; not a night had gone by that she did not get to sing her baby boy to sleep. She had her son back—it was too good to be true.

And yet, it was, wasn't it?

As the baby was handed back into her arms that afternoon in the Egyptian sun, no sooner had she pressed him against her chest than a deal had been made.

He's yours, for now. Bring him back, and I will raise him as my own.

She rocked and hugged him, and the tears came again.

The tears of a mother are ever-ready. The tears change, but they always come. After she allowed the lament to sink in . . . had it been an hour already? . . . Moses slept in her arms. Jochebed coached her soul, "I trusted God with my boy in a river; I will trust God with my boy in a palace." She repeated her prayer, her plea, her resolve, over and over. Back and forth she rocked, repeating her trust.

She would trust God. *He is faithful. He is good. He will rescue us.*

Again, she had no idea she held the answer to her prayer in her arms.

———

Shiphrah, Puah, Jochebed, Miriam, Pharaoh's daughter.

All five women rebelled against Pharaoh in her own way. Each woman spread her maternal wings like a mother hen, protecting Moses, the one who would lead the entire Hebrew nation out of slavery from Pharaoh. This community of women pioneered the way to freedom, long before Moses's sandals hit the dry bottom of the Red Sea.

Are you overwhelmed by your circumstances? Shiphrah and Puah were, too. But they made sure to do one thing in this hard place: honor God. And He honored them. Ask God how to honor Him in this moment. He will lead you. He is a good shepherd.

Are you sending off a child to kindergarten or college, or releasing a project into the world? Jochebed knows your pain of taking your hands off the basket and trusting God with your heart floating downriver. Of what it means to let go of control. But God's hands will hold your child when you let go. God's hands will handle the outcomes of your hard work. Your child started in His hands, and He knows what they need. His love is stronger than anything you can imagine.

Are you young in your faith and feel in over your head? Miriam did, too. But she looked for opportunities to be faithful. And God was with her all the way.

Is your heart changing and shifting from what you've been taught about others, softening to the injustice around you? Are you asking how you can leverage any privilege you've been handed? Pharaoh's daughter let herself soften. And it was beautiful.

It took a village to raise Moses. Five women, to be exact. But I had never known their names until recently. These diamonds in the rough each played a significant role in the rescue and raising of the man who spoke to God face-to-face, like a friend (see Exodus 33:11). A man who, though timid and tongue-tied, obeyed God and challenged Pharaoh to let God's people go and worship Him. Who was quite afraid to do this all alone, and God gave him his brother by his side, after his sister had secured his well-being years before. Who raised his hands and God parted the seas through him. Who was given the Ten Commandments.

Let's raise a glass to the ezers—the daughters—who bravely obeyed God rather than man. And birthed one of the most influential leaders in Israelite history.

4

The Womb

We Have Bodies That Belong

Can a mother forget the baby at her breast and have no compassion on the child she has borne? Though she may forget, I will not forget you! See, I have engraved you on the palms of my hands; your walls are ever before me.

Isaiah 49:15–16

Did you know the first quality God assigns to Himself is of being compassionate? Me neither, until recently. I am not sure how I missed it (well, this ADHD girl misses a lot, actually, so there's that), but now I can't unsee it. After a friend casually said to me, "God is compassion-forward," her words rolled around my head for a few days like one of those tiny metal balls inside a handheld plastic maze. I was trying to work that idea out.

And true to form, I had questions. Is God really compassion-forward? What does that even mean? What does it mean to be compassionate?

It didn't take me long to find out. A few chapters after our five women rescued baby Moses, God and now-adult Moses were having a moment on top of Mount Sinai. God passed in front of Moses and called out:

> Yahweh! The LORD!
>   The God of compassion and mercy!
> I am slow to anger
>   and filled with unfailing love and faithfulness.
>
> Exodus 34:6 NLT

The God of Compassion

And I had never really seen it before. So often, in our earliest iterations of faith, we might categorize God as angry in the Old Testament and gracious in the New Testament. We can often drift toward binary terms, black and white, good or bad, angry or kind. But the more time we spend in God's presence and understand His Word, a fuller, more robust picture emerges, and from faith to faith we go.

In just the second book of the Bible, right after the book of Genesis (meaning *beginning*), God reveals His character to Moses. And then for centuries it is this very monumental mountain moment that the poets and the prophets call back upon. Aspects of this fivefold character of God are repeated as somewhat of a refrain at least twelve other times (Numbers 14:18, Nehemiah 9:17, Nehemiah 13:22, Psalm 5:7–8, Psalm 69:16, Psalm 86:5, Psalm 86:15; Psalm 103:8, Psalm 145:8, Isaiah 63:7, Joel 2:13, Jonah 4:2).

God is compassionate, gracious, slow to anger, and abounding with unfailing love and faithfulness.

What a gift we have in the character of God!

And for us daughters, the gift keeps giving. In the BibleProject podcast episode "The Womb of God," Carissa Quinn says, "The Hebrew word is 'rakhum' and it comes in a verb form, a noun form, an adjective form. But the really fascinating thing about all of them is that they're related to the word 'rekhem,' which is the Hebrew word for 'womb.'"[1]

The nurturing nature of God? I hadn't ever heard a sermon on this idea of God's compassion being related to a womb. I'm about to state the obvious, but let's just spell it out for kicks. Only a woman has a womb (thank you for coming to my science class). God's first characteristic He calls out for Moses is a quality that gives us all the momma bear vibes. Like the first time my son was pushed down on the playground by an older child, and I immediately stood up from the park bench and was ready to rescue, to fight, to protect, to defend him. My inner ezer, as a lifeguard, was in full force. And this knee-jerk reaction was part of it.

Of course compassion is not only a feminine quality. But a womb is. The place where life is grown and protected, nourished and safe. By naming this quality, God honors His daughters and their bodies. He honors our wombs, whether we bear physical children or not. He honors our bodies—our beautiful, life-giving, resilient, wondrous bodies. Whether they physically give birth or spiritually provide protection or emotionally give support, our bodies are meaningful and purposeful. Our bodies are good and needed. Our bodies are unique and belong in the redemptive story of God.

I love how author Jess Connolly puts it in *Breaking Free from Body Shame*:

> My body is good. God made it with intention and creativity. I believe He knew before the world began what I would look like. The first name that was given to my body by God was

definitive: good. I believe He makes good things, and I believe that because He created my body, it is a good creation.[2]

So praise God for the goodness of our bodies. And also for the unique proximity the words *womb* and *compassion* have in Hebrew. They are so closely tied, so related. But when it comes to God's compassion? His surpasses a woman's compassion every day of the week. Why? Because God's compassion is never contingent upon our behavior.

For years, my compassion had been tied to how someone was behaving toward me. I was a master at conditional compassion. I would move toward you with empathy if you stayed kind. But the minute you came at me? I grabbed my boxing gloves and climbed into the ring. Or to mix metaphors, I took up a sword, not a cross. This issue came to a head in my motherhood. I realized I had no room for the big emotions, big fears, big anxieties inside the ever-changing body of a middle schooler. Also, just to be clear, no matter what size the middle schooler is, those emotions are so much bigger than they know how to handle. But I couldn't keep perspective, and my compassion would run out faster than Gatorade at a football practice in July in Ohio. When my kids needed compassion, I brought shame. And that wasn't the kind of mother I wanted to be.

This is why I am beyond grateful that God's compassion is not like mine. His mothering compassion is next level. And it always has been. Which sounds vaguely familiar, yes? From Moses to the Messiah—the message has been that we cannot prove ourselves worthy of God's love and compassion. We cannot earn God's compassion. He just bestows it upon us because of who He is, not because of who we are. His compassion is not contingent on how sassy we are or how emotional we are or how fickle we are. Or how good we are or how trusting we are or how prayerful we are. We see in Nehemiah 9:27–28:

> So you delivered them into the hands of their enemies, who oppressed them. But when they were oppressed they cried out to you. From heaven you heard them, and in your great compassion you gave them deliverers, who rescued them from the hand of their enemies. But as soon as they were at rest, they again did what was evil in your sight. Then you abandoned them to the hand of their enemies so that they ruled over them. And when they cried out to you again, you heard from heaven, and in your compassion you delivered them time after time.

Tim Mackie points out that "the moral quality, the character quality, of the people crying out doesn't seem to matter. . . . God always listens. . . . God's people are constantly turning away from Him, but somehow, he's always able to find a way to have compassion on them. . . ." Carissa Quinn says, "This is a really amazing characteristic of God to depend on. We can know what His disposition is when we cry out to Him."[3]

When we turn our backs on Him, His face is still turned toward us because of His great womb-like compassion. Like a mother who sees the vulnerability, immaturity, and needs of her child and cannot help but to move in close and care. Yet even a human mother may neglect her vulnerable child, but not God.

> Can a mother forget the baby at her breast and have no compassion on the child she has borne? Though she may forget, I will not forget you! See, I have engraved you on the palms of my hands; your walls are ever before me.
>
> Isaiah 49:15–16

God is described here as a nursing mother. One who provides sustenance from her very own resilient and amazing body, who has the privilege of holding her child a few inches from her face as she feeds her baby, whose entire body responds with a tingling sensation, letting down milk, when her child cries. One who will not sleep. One who will use her strength to sustain the weak. One who sacrifices so much so that her baby has enough.

Is it possible I was much more like God than I ever thought as I woke from a fevered sleep to the cry of my child, sleep-walked down the hall, groggily picked up my hungry and dirty-diapered infant—my shirt wet from both sweat and fresh milk—and nursed my baby in the dead of night? Is it possible that I bore God's image most beautifully when my whole body turned toward my crying baby? Is it likely that I looked like Yahweh, rising once again and moving in so close to take care of my child's never-ending needs? I believe so.

And we see this image more places in Isaiah:

> For a long time I have kept silent, I have been quiet and held myself back. But now, like a woman in childbirth, I cry out, I gasp and pant.
>
> Isaiah 42:14

> As a mother comforts her child, so will I comfort you; and you will be comforted over Jerusalem.
>
> Isaiah 66:13

And that's not all when it comes to the mother heart of God.

We also see an image in the Psalms of a mother bird, who uses her wings to hide, to protect, to be a refuge for, and to cover her babies. Shiao Chong shares the following verses as examples and states, "Jesus picks up these images when he laments over Jerusalem."[4]

> Keep me as the apple of your eye; hide me in the shadow of your wings.
>
> Psalm 17:8

> . . . I will take refuge in the shadow of your wings until the disaster has passed.
>
> Psalm 57:1

> He will cover you with his feathers, and under his wings you will find refuge . . .
>
> Psalm 91:4

Jesus echoes this sentiment, longing to gather his children like a hen gathering her chicks, pulling them close, keeping them safe, nurturing their bodies and souls:

> Jerusalem, Jerusalem, you who kill the prophets and stone those sent to you, how often I have longed to gather your children together, as a hen gathers her chicks under her wings, and you were not willing.
>
> Matthew 23:37 and Luke 13:34

I must admit I have been surprised and have wondered why I haven't heard the themes of God's womb, his maternal wings, his momma bear heart for us before. Why haven't I heard this reflection of God? This maternal side? This womb-like compassion? And why haven't I seen the supremacy of His compassion, far above ours? How His compassion is better and different from ours, rising up in the face of our own rebellion? Why hadn't I seen Jesus's deep and guttural response—as Jerusalem had stoned the very prophets God sent before Him—to not stone them back, but to gather them close like a mother? And why haven't I seen all the ways Paul himself compares himself to a mother, and a nursing mother at that? In 1 Thessalonians 2:7 (ESV), he writes, "We were gentle among you, like a nursing mother taking care of her own children" (see also Galatians 4:19, 2 Thessalonians 3:8–9, 1 Corinthians 3:2).

Even as the wombs of women reflect God's compassion, His compassion exceeds ours. We may forget our children, but He will never forget. We may want to reject our children because of their behavior, but God longs to gather His children—destructive as they may be—close. His compassionate ways are much higher than our compassionate ways (see Isaiah 55:6–9).

The beauty of God's compassion woven through Scripture may have been passed over for a variety reasons. But I am finding that the more women we have studying Scripture, the more women find themselves in the story. Here's what I know now: I am committed to no longer being surprised by God's character in this way. The show notes for the BibleProject podcast "The Womb of God?" put it best: "Both man and woman reflect God's image and likeness, so we shouldn't be surprised when these feminine depictions are used to describe the character of God."[5]

Daughter, if God has these feminine depictions, then we can take heart. We, as women, are made in the image of a God who aches to gather younger ones close to Him. And this compassionate care can come in a million forms, by the way. This isn't just about mothers having wombs. This is about daughters having a God who feels what they feel. If you have ever had a response to protect someone, you are like God. If you have ever stepped in to defend another, you are like God. If you have ever used what power and privilege you have to speak up for others, you are like God. If you have ever fed others, welcomed them in, opened your arms to hug someone hurting, you are like God.

But maybe this deep dive into compassion and wombs is hard to swallow. Oh, friend, I know this can bring up pain and deep frustration. I slogged through years of infertility, years of feeling less than in a church culture that can often elevate motherhood to an inappropriate place. Where the subtle prize seems to be being a wife and a mom instead of being a beloved daughter of the Most High King. In my struggle with wanting to become a mother, I wondered why I was *this* kind of broken, and not a different kind. For years my body wasn't able to get pregnant, and when I finally did, my baby came six weeks early and had a NICU stay and path I hadn't expected that first year. Why didn't my body cooperate with me? I didn't have answers. And I still don't. But I have a blessing to offer you:

May the God of Compassion wash over you with His warm love and unending grace right now. May you know He sees you, is for you, is empathizing with your weaknesses and your frailty and your frustration. May you know that being His daughter is enough. To be loved by Him is enough. To be known by Him is enough. To be seen by Him is enough. He hears your longing. He is working in your aching. And your story is not done yet. Amen.

5

The Prophet

We Have Voices That Belong

Hilkiah the priest, Ahikam, Akbor, Shaphan and Asaiah went to speak to the prophet Huldah, who was the wife of Shallum son of Tikvah, the son of Harhas, keeper of the wardrobe. She lived in Jerusalem, in the New Quarter.

2 Kings 22:14

There was a guy named Shallum who was a keeper of the king's wardrobe. Which sounds like a job I would absolutely be down for. Making sure the king was looking fly? I'm in. I've been a sucker for fashion for most of my life. Including my College Thrift Shop Era (I worked three jobs and was still barely making rent, so I had to be thrifty), during which I found some 1970s gems and paired them with my favorite pink corduroy pants and these wing-tipped brown and turquoise chunky shoes with a subtle lacy pattern resembling a fancy cookie. Soon, that was one of my nicknames. Fancy Cookie. I wore this outfit while I rode my purple scooter on campus. The kind with the eight-inch tires from the '80s, not the scooters with the little fast wheels you see now. I know. If you only knew me then.

Anyway, Shallum, on top of his fantastic fashion job, also had a wife named Huldah.

Who?

My question, too. Let's step into King Josiah's palace and see who she was.

King Josiah looked down at his torn robes, his tears leaving dried salty patches on his cheeks. Running his fingers through his hair, he paced in front of his throne. Everything was a mess. They had disobeyed God's ways, they had worshiped other idols, they had polluted the land in a thousand ways. His stomach turned, despair filling him instead of dinner. His tears were his food.

Ever since the Torah had been discovered when he ordered the cleaning of the temple, his heart had been wrung out like a sponge. He winced at every word Shaphan read. The entire nation had collectively spit upon the covenant the God of Abraham made with them. For decades.

"God forgive us, cleanse us, restore us, speak to us," King Josiah murmured.

What now? Where should he turn? What could be done? He needed discernment, perspective, something. He needed a prophet.

King Josiah knew who the prophets were in the land. He had five choices: Jeremiah, Zephaniah, Nahum, Habakkuk, and Huldah.[1]

And as the king, the most powerful leader in the land, he would naturally summon one of the prophets to come to him.[2] The highest in rank always had home court advantage.

But uncovering this book had undone his soul. He humbled himself, wept in grief at the sins of Israel, tore his clothing in lament, and emptied himself of all kingly glory. Laying aside his crown, he wouldn't demand a prophet come to him. He would humbly send his best men to the best prophet.

Huldah.

––––––––––

Her hands worked effortlessly, grinding grain. Her cocoa-colored hair tied back and out of her face, she wiped her brow with the back of her hand. This was the third hour she had been working to make flour.[3] Soon she would take a break, stretch, and hydrate before she would gather her fresh flour to start bread.

Huldah and her husband worked hard, forearms and fingers sore from their daily tasks. They handled anything from Levite priestly wardrobe fabric to all matters of food and sustenance.[4]

Some days she found herself lost in her tasks, hands working, mind wandering. Today, her senses were heightened. Almost as if she smelled a fresh resolve in the air, a restoration, a renewal. The way her bedroom felt when she changed the sheets, swept the floor, opened the blinds to the view of the strong, protective Jerusalem wall. The scent of freshness swirled. Their humble home was inside the city wall, an ezer of protection, close to the king's quarters. Was the north wind bringing this shift, this sense, from the direction of King Josiah's courts? What an oddly specific imagination she had sometimes.

Looking down at her finely ground grain-turned-flour, she marveled yet again at the making of it. The way her grandmother and mother had done. And from such dust came new life—bread, nourishment, satisfaction. The way the story of old went: the God of Abraham crafting humans from dust. Grain had to be pressed, broken down, crushed before the bread came. Only after the grinding came the goodness.

The firm knock on her juniper door startled her out of her thoughts. She jumped, then steadied her breath. *Great.* She looked down at the floured handprint on her chest. *Unexpected company, and I look like I lost a fistfight with a flour sack.*

"Just a moment!" she called. Wiping off her apron, she looked around to see if anything should be shoved elsewhere. Sometimes her husband absentmindedly left a trail behind him of sweaty work clothes. God bless Shallum. He was a good man.

Things looked decent enough as she approached the doorway. But she heard not only one voice but a few. Maybe three? Four? And all low in tone . . . all male? Why would a small group of men gather at her door without warning? And did she have enough wine and challah for her surprise guests? Her brain quickly ran through her pantry as she surveyed the olives and cheeses in her mind's eye. Should be enough.

She opened the door.

Hilkiah the priest, Ahikam, Akbor, Shaphan and Asaiah went to speak to the prophet Huldah, who was the wife of Shallum son of Tikvah, the son of Harhas, keeper of the wardrobe. She lived in Jerusalem, in the New Quarter.

She said to them, "This is what the LORD, the God of Israel, says: Tell the man who sent you to me, 'This is what the LORD says: I am going to bring disaster on this place and its people, according to everything written in the book the king of Judah has read. Because they have forsaken me and burned incense to other gods and aroused my anger by all the idols their hands have made, my anger will burn against this place and will not be quenched.' Tell the king of Judah, who sent you to inquire of the LORD, 'This is what the LORD, the God of Israel, says concerning the words you heard: Because your heart was responsive and you humbled yourself before the LORD when you heard what I have spoken against this place and its people—that they would become a curse and be laid waste—and because you tore your robes and wept in my presence, I also have heard you, declares the LORD. Therefore I will gather you to your ancestors, and you will be buried in peace. Your eyes will not see all the disaster I am going to bring on this place.'"

So they took her answer back to the king.

2 Kings 22:14–20

She stood in her kitchen, mind racing. Huldah, in her own home, had just boldly proclaimed the word of God, speaking with authority, declaring blessings and curses over Israel to take back to King Josiah.

She was keenly aware she was a prophet and had given prophecies in the past. But this time—it was for the king himself. The king had sent his men to her; he had not summoned her to himself. What respect and honor and privilege she just experienced! And the prophecy just poured out of her mouth like a robust aged wine into heirloom glasses at a wedding.

But this felt more like a funeral. Why couldn't she have given a cute, sweet, fluffy encouragement about the king's vats of wine being filled to overflowing and his cheese boards never running out? Sigh. This was not that.

Israel had forsaken the God of Israel, and disaster would come. The idols ignited God's anger, and He was displeased in every way.

And yet . . . she had sensed a shift right before they arrived. The shift was the king's repentant heart, his cleaning of the temple, his obedience and softness to God's ways. And for that, he would know peace.

She was exhausted. Time for a nap. Prophesying took it out of her.

She remembered her mother. Her mother—since Huldah was a young girl—had always said she was a leader, willing to say the hard thing no matter what. She was strong and sturdy, like a pillar in a palace. The way King David blessed Israel's daughters: "May our sons in their youth be like plants full grown, our daughters like corner pillars cut for the structure of a palace" (Psalm 144:12 ESV). She had stood tall and strong to bring God's word to the palace. *May God be honored, and to Him be the glory.*

What Josiah had set in motion—restoring the temple and clearing away the idols—was further fueled by calling upon Huldah to hear from the Lord. Christa L. McKirland notes,

> Upon hearing from his envoys about the word of the Lord, Josiah acted immediately by calling all of God's people together and requiring their devotion to the God of their fathers (2 Kings 23). The king did not delay, seek a second opinion, nor dismiss Huldah's words because she was a woman. Instead, this righteous king—full of wisdom, discernment, and spiritual sensitivity—sought to return to the covenant as an indication of his devotion to Yahweh—despite the fact that the damage was irrevocable, and the judgment final. Josiah, a rare example of a righteous king and obedient leader, submitted to the authoritative word of God communicated by a woman. We see his righteousness through this narrative. Even in response to this dismal oracle, his devotion persisted. Despite an inevitable judgment, Josiah instituted national reform in conformity to the covenant of Yahweh, based on the confirmation and interpretation of the Book of the Law by Huldah.[5]

Sure enough, God speaks through His daughters.

Huldah was truly a strong pillar, a metaphorical fixture in King Josiah's palace. Even though she did not step foot inside those walls, her prophecy was a pillar in the palace. What an incredible witness and honor she was given. And this was not just from any king. The text records that "there was no king like him, who turned to the LORD with all his heart and with all his soul and with all his might, according to all the Law of Moses" (2 Kings 23:25 ESV).

King Josiah decided to break generational sin and cycles of idol worship that had gone before him under many kings past. And, it seems, he broke the pattern of only consulting male prophets, too. As McKirland wonders, "In the same way that women were the first to testify to the resurrection of Christ, the living Word, how poetic might it be that the first person to authenticate the written Word might also have been a woman?"[6] Josiah had recognized the book as the word of God, but Huldah certainly confirmed it.

In light of Huldah's prophecy and faithfulness, we can answer the question Scot McKnight asks—"What did women do?"—when it comes to God's daughters in the Bible and in the ministry of the life of the church: They prophesied. They spoke for God. They were called upon to speak into the future of the kingdom of God. They used their voices. And they did much more. McKnight writes:

> [King Josiah] chooses the female prophet, Huldah, above the rest. Huldah is not chosen because no men were available; she is chosen because she is truly exceptional among the prophets. She confirms that the scroll is indeed God's Torah and this, in some sense, authorizes this text as Israel's Scriptures from this time on.[7]

And you, sister, can be a pillar who speaks with confidence as you listen to what God is saying. You can raise your voice of encouragement, of truth, of prophecy, of discernment, of knowledge, of wisdom, of hope, of love. You have been given a voice to use, not to hide.

Humility crowns King Josiah's head in this era. And because of it, a woman is sought, the nation is called to repent, and the tide is turned. Part of their repentance was returning to the rhythms they had neglected, which included Passover. And so the most memorable king threw the most memorable party in Israel's history. "There had not been a

Passover celebration like that since the time when the judges ruled in Israel, nor throughout all the years of the kings of Israel and Judah" (2 Kings 23:22 NLT). I feel quite partial to King Josiah; he repents hard and parties hard.

If we were to play the icebreaker game Never Have I Ever, I would hold up five fingers and say Never Have I Ever heard a sermon on Huldah. Never have I ever heard about how five of the king's men came to her, instead of the king summoning a prophet to come to him. I have not ever heard of her boldness, her prophecy, and her authority, which Rev. Olga and Rev. Stephen Shaffer say came "with the same Spirit of boldness that filled Peter when he proclaimed the word of God to the leaders of Israel, proclaiming the need to obey God rather than humans (Acts 4:19, 5:29)."[8]

Huldah has given me permission to use my voice. In spaces where I was unsure of when it was my turn to speak, where I was surveying the room to see if I was going to be invited to say something or if I was going to have to bravely step in, I would think of Huldah. It is clear she had attuned her heart to God's heart. Huldah knew God's character. And Huldah knew who she was as His daughter. So when the time came, she spoke. Not timidly, not with excuses or I'm sorrys, but with confidence in her God. Her boldness came from her God. And so does mine. So does yours.

Huldah's gifts are woven into the tapestry of King Josiah's lineage. And for her boldness and authority, I honor her and stand on her shoulders. She may only have a paragraph in the pages of the Old Testament, but her impact had a ripple effect on the nation of Israel for years to come. As daughters in her wake, may we follow her footsteps, speak the truth in love, and stand as pillars of the palace in the kingdom of God. And may God be glorified.

6

The Oaks

We Belong in God's Soil

But I am like an olive tree
    flourishing in the house of God;
I trust in God's unfailing love
    for ever and ever.

Psalm 52:8

Our daughter's name is ripe with meaning.

When we realized we were having a daughter, I felt paralyzed by the unending possibilities. What name could we possibly choose that encompassed all of my dreams for my only daughter? What if she hated her name when she was older? What if it became trendy—like Amy in the '80s—and she had five of them in her homeroom? (Ahem, that was me.) What if it was too unique and people commented on it incessantly and awkwardly? What if it was not fun to write out in bubble letters when she was bored during science class?

This is the weight of naming a daughter. Waffling between "it's just a name" to "her name is everything."

We entered the hospital with two names at the top of the list. We thought we would know the second we saw her. She was unnamed for twelve hours.

After hours of labor, she was finally nestled on my chest. I held her, teary, exhausted, sweaty, covered in all kinds of who-knows-what liquid. The long haul of birth was over, and there was our little girl, beautiful and healthy.

I turned to my husband in exhaustion and sighed. "Can you just decide? Just name her." I think I was also falling asleep, my question slurring its way out of my mouth. I was tired of making decisions. Just make the call.

"Let's just wait until you're rested. There's no rush. It's her name."

I love him. So kind, patient, steady. Like an immovable oak tree. Not easily swayed by his bone-tired wife's demands— believing I really did care about a name, even if in the moment all I cared about was closing my eyelids and checking off the "Named Her" box. Bringing life into the world takes the life right out of you.

He was right. Sleep births perspective.

A few hours later my husband squeezed into my hospital bed, gently shoving me over in the tiny twin bed, to lie next to me. All we did was stare at her in silence. A baby girl. A little gem. A precious soul.

The nurse came in and asked, "So, do we have a name for Baby Girl Seiffert?"

"Not yet," my husband replied. "Still thinking."

"Ooohhhhkay," the nurse replied as she walked out. Was she judging our lack of naming skills? Or the fact that my husband wiggled his way into my hospital bed that wasn't made for two?

As the nurse closed the door and we admired our girl's full head of jet-black hair and her perfect red lips, I said, "I think she looks like an Olive."

"Me too," he whispered.

And so she was named. Olive. With that wonderful round capital O she could script as big and as perfect as she'd like when signing checks or her books. And the meaning was my favorite: beauty, dignity, and fruitfulness. Like a tall, strong oak tree.

God is a gardener, through and through. One of the first things God does at the very beginning of time as we know it? He plants a garden. Can you picture it? God, kneeling in the soil, getting His hands dirty, pushing it around and placing it just so, speaking kindly to His little saplings. He is Creator God, sowing, watering, tending, pruning, growing. God has the ultimate green thumb—from hostas to humans, He is the Perfect Gardener.

> Now the Lord God had planted a garden in the east, in Eden; and there he put the man he had formed. The Lord God made all kinds of trees grow out of the ground—trees that were pleasing to the eye and good for food. In the middle of the garden were the tree of life and the tree of the knowledge of good and evil.
>
> Genesis 2:8–9

He planted a garden and then breathed His own breath into Adam and then commissioned human beings to image Him and to care for the earth (see Genesis 1:26–31 and 2:7). To tend to the leaves, check the soil, water the dirt, prune what wasn't serving the plants any longer. We garden in His image, and He called both men and women to the task.

And we, too, are His garden.

In the famous messianic text in Isaiah—the one Jesus stands up in the synagogue and quotes as being fulfilled in their hearing—God names us His very own trees.

> They will be called oaks of righteousness,
> a planting of the LORD
> for the display of his splendor.
>
> They will rebuild the ancient ruins
> and restore the places long devastated;
> they will renew the ruined cities
> that have been devastated for generations.
> Strangers will shepherd your flocks;
> foreigners will work your fields and vineyards.
> And you will be called priests of the LORD,
> you will be named ministers of our God.
>
> Isaiah 61:3–6

I have been drawn to this text for years. And lately, I keep coming back to it as an identity marker. Specifically as God's daughter.

We will be called oaks of righteousness, the planting of the Lord, for the display of His splendor.

So often I wrestle with what others have called me. Or not called me. Or what I think they believe I should do or be, where I should go or stay. Some seasons I have allowed myself to be shaped by what others think of me, instead of what my Creator thinks of me as His daughter. Isaiah is clear about who has planted us, whose hands have made us. As oaks of righteousness, we are planted by God and for God. And oaks are full of life. A planting of the Lord. It is God who has planned us and planted us with specific care, tending to every comma and period of our story. We are the saplings of His hands. We aren't in the care of a human gardener; we are in the hands of the Divine Vine Dresser Himself.

But sometimes we daughters forget. Sometimes what others have called us has rung louder than the call God has made on our lives. And we have only rehearsed the voices of others, quieting the voice of our Father. But the more secure we are in God's love, the less insecure in the world we will be. The more rooted in God's compassion for us we are, the more established we will be. In fact, this is Paul's prayer for the church—to be the firmly rooted, tall, and strong oaks Isaiah told us we were: "And I pray that you, being rooted and established in love, may have power, together with all the Lord's holy people, to grasp how wide and long and high and deep is the love of Christ . . ." (Ephesians 3:17–18).

God's daughters are deeply, fiercely loved. With a width and length and height and depth that we must remember often and stand planted securely in. God took a special moment in the garden to put Adam to sleep so He could carefully build us as ezers (Eve). And God sees His daughters (Hagar). He hears us pour out our prayers (Hannah). He gives us courage to fight for justice and righteousness (Puah and Shiphrah). He honors our ingenuity and grit (Jochebed). He commissions us to lead (Deborah). He calls us to be worship leaders, writing songs and leading others into praise (Miriam). He widens the table for those of us who are immigrants, the sojourners, the foreigners—*and if we aren't Jewish, that's us* (Ruth). He guards those who testify to His wonders (Rahab). He reveals deep truths to us (the Samaritan woman). He defends the abused (the adulterous woman). He encourages us to learn like His disciples (Mary). He blesses us in our tears (Mary). He takes care of us in the darkest times (Mary, the mother of Jesus at the cross). He sends us out to share the good news (Mary Magdalene). He calls us to lead churches (Nympha). He moves us to teach others (Priscilla). He honors every kind of ministry we might have (Romans 16). And those are just a few examples.

And let's note that this call is a *communal call*. We are oaks (plural) of righteousness, standing side by side, both men and women, who are from every tongue, tribe, and nation, people with every kind of melanin and lack thereof, every kind of language, every kind of hindrance and weakness and fragility, every kind of background and bruise, every kind of perspective and dream, all being gardened by the Master Gardener Himself.

And we display *His* splendor, not ours. Our strong, sturdy trunks—learning to bend and not break under the pressures of life, the stress of life, the anxiety of people pleasing, the darkness of fear, the wind of uncertainty—are to display His splendor and glory. We are made by the Gardener, for the Gardener. Not to be abused or misused by man, not to further someone else's splendid agenda, not to hustle for our worth in an exhausted and overworked world. No, we are oaks—who bring rightness where there are wrongs—named by a compassionate, gracious, slow-to-prune Gardener. Called to drop acorns of love, joy, peace, patience, kindness, goodness, faithfulness, gentleness, and self-control. The fruit of the Spirit of God inside of us.

———

A good gardener doesn't plant a garden and then turn on his heel and walk away. A good gardener tends to the garden daily, trains it on sturdy structures if needed, prunes back what is dying, considers the soil, and adjusts. In the same way, God has been tending to our souls from the beginning and will tend them to the end.

Just as the curse began in a garden, so does the redemption. Just as a daughter took the fruit that unraveled the blessing, another daughter took the firstfruits of good news to restore it. Just as the first humans were banned from the first garden, the first of the resurrection welcomed us back into it.

That first resurrection morning, Mary was weeping at the tomb of Jesus. And as she was crying, someone was standing there with her.

> Now Mary stood outside the tomb crying. As she wept, she bent over to look into the tomb and saw two angels in white, seated where Jesus' body had been, one at the head and the other at the foot.
>
> They asked her, "Woman, why are you crying?"
>
> "They have taken my Lord away," she said, "and I don't know where they have put him." At this, she turned around and saw Jesus standing there, but she did not realize that it was Jesus.
>
> He asked her, "Woman, why are you crying? Who is it you are looking for?"
>
> Thinking he was the gardener, she said, "Sir, if you have carried him away, tell me where you have put him, and I will get him."
>
> Jesus said to her, "Mary."
>
> She turned toward him and cried out in Aramaic, "Rabboni!" (which means "Teacher").
>
> John 20:11–16

Thinking he was the gardener.

I have zero doubt that the Holy Spirit, through John, penned that observation on purpose. Disguised as a gardener, whether blurred through tears or hidden by the Spirit, the man before Mary was one she could only imagine was a gardener in front of her, asking her who she was looking for.

And Jesus tends to her soul in this moment—and ours. This is a tender and personal moment for Mary. And a grandiose, metanarrative plot twist for the most glorious story ever written. Back in Eden, surrounded by every kind of fruit tree imaginable, blessing was pronounced. But then the curse was announced and the garden was closed.

But on this first Easter morning, surrounded by death and tombs, new life was pronounced. The stone was rolled away, and the garden was opened to us all. Easter tells us Eden is being restored.

Where there was hiding in the first garden, there was seeking in the second. After Adam and Eve ate the fruit, they hid their bodies from one another in shame, and they hid from God. But in the garden tomb this first resurrection morning, Mary did the exact opposite. Instead of hiding, she ran toward Jesus, ran toward fellowship, ran toward Him with every ounce of her being without shame or anything to hinder her. She—His daughter—had to get to Jesus.

———

Just a few days before Jesus was killed and rose again, he taught the disciples about the Holy Spirit, the Advocate to come. The one who would teach us, guide us, and give us what we need when we need it (see John 14–16). And right in the middle of His comfort and encouragement, Jesus gave us a picture:

> I am the true vine, and my Father is the gardener. He cuts off every branch in me that bears no fruit, while every branch that does bear fruit he prunes so that it will be even more

fruitful. You are already clean because of the word I have spoken to you. Remain in me, as I also remain in you. No branch can bear fruit by itself; it must remain in the vine. Neither can you bear fruit unless you remain in me. I am the vine; you are the branches. If you remain in me and I in you, you will bear much fruit; apart from me you can do nothing. If you do not remain in me, you are like a branch that is thrown away and withers; such branches are picked up, thrown into the fire and burned. If you remain in me and my words remain in you, ask whatever you wish, and it will be done for you. This is to my Father's glory, that you bear much fruit, showing yourselves to be my disciples.

John 15:1–8

Daughter, you have a good Father who is a Master Gardener. And Jesus wants you to remain, abide, stay connected, make your abode in your Father. You and I are His delightful branches, and we belong in Him. And why must we stay connected? Disconnected branches die. And Jesus came to bring us life to the fullest. So we must attune ourselves to God often, turn our attention to Him throughout our days, stay at home with Him. As women, so much is competing for our attention. The lists, the needs, the relationships, the caretaking, the worries, the emails, the permission slips, the bills, the car payments, the emotional wellness of those around us.

But our connection to our Creator is vital. God does not want His daughters to bear the fruit of exhaustion and pride and anxiety. He desires us to bear the fruit of faith and hope and love. He does not want us to produce the fruit of fear and insecurity and bitterness. He wants us to bear the fruit of joy and peace and goodness. He wants us to simply abide, to belong, to be His. To turn our attention often to the Spirit of God inside of us and whisper, "What's next, Papa?" (Romans

8:15 MSG). And in being His, He will produce the fruit, and we will drop acorns of righteousness into our unjust world. How do we know? "But the fruit of the Spirit is love, joy, peace, forbearance, kindness, goodness, faithfulness, gentleness and self-control. Against such things there is no law" (Galatians 5:22–23).

Daughter, may you make your home in the garden, tended to by your Father Gardener. May you practice turning your attention to God's Spirit inside you, gardening your precious soul. May you not stay hidden when you sin but run to the compassionate arms of Jesus in your need. May you remember the deep, affectionate, fierce love of the daughters of the past. May you cease striving to produce fruit that rots but bear fruit that lasts in the kingdom of God. May you do the work of staying connected and attentive to God—to your source of life, of rest, of restoration, of redemption.

7

The Heroes

We Belong with Our Leadership

> Because he had nine hundred chariots fitted with iron and had cruelly oppressed the Israelites for twenty years, they cried to the LORD for help. Now Deborah, a prophet, the wife of Lappidoth, was leading Israel at that time. She held court under the Palm of Deborah between Ramah and Bethel in the hill country of Ephraim, and the Israelites went up to her to have their disputes decided.
>
> Judges 4:3–5

My mom's name is Deborah. And she loves herself some palm trees. In fact, we would drive the eighteen hours from Toledo, Ohio, to Galveston, Texas, several summers in a row for vacation. After 153 snacks, one too many license plate games, and my parents' road trip music, including The Traveling Wilburys and The Who, we uncoiled ourselves from the back seat and stepped into palm tree land. It was vacation time.

I want you to meet a different Deborah with a different palm tree going on. She has a slightly different vibe than my mom (think more swords than sandy pink toes), but she did settle disputes and dropped some knowledge like my mom often did. Deborah was one of Israel's judges, and her leadership is fascinating.

"Nine hundred iron chariots?!" The women whispered to one another as they bought spices and surveyed figs and olives at the market. What did that even mean? What does an iron chariot look like? Who designed that, and how long did it take to forge?

"Have you heard about Jabin, king of Canaan? He has horses with iron chariots—and nine hundred of them!" The men murmured at the city gates, fear rising, considering what kind of cost and resources it took to make iron chariots. Surely this was the end of them.

"Oh Lord, God of Abraham, rescue us! We have been oppressed for twenty years! We see how our sin and our evil have brought us under this tyranny, but we ask that through your great compassion you would deliver us. . . ." Levite priests prayed, begging God to rescue them late at night.

The whispers throughout the nation of Israel were growing louder. The rumors turned into prayers that turned into lament. *How long, O Lord, will we be slaves in Canaan under Jabin? And now the commander of the Canaanite army, Sisera, has created an army of iron? We are helpless, we are sunk! Save us, O God.*

The cries of God's people have always stirred God's compassion. Like a mother's milk lets down when her infant cries, God's gut response is to move toward the oppressed and to help. Even when the people's own sin brought on the oppression, God's compassion never left. It's who He is, as He told

Moses: compassionate, gracious, slow to anger, abounding in loving kindness and faithfulness (see Exodus 34:6).

And did you catch the way the story unfolds in the beginning of the chapter? ". . . [T]hey cried to the Lord for help. Now Deborah, a prophet, the wife of Lappidoth, was leading Israel at that time" (Judges 4:3–4). Israel cried out to God for help, and a mother showed up. Like moms do. Deborah, the prophet and judge, is here. She is, in fact, referred to as "a mother in Israel" in Judges 5:7. Deborah is placed here by God, ready to help and respond and lead in the face of the coming battle. Like an ezer, bearing God's image, Deborah is ready. She has been there this whole time, under her palm tree, holding court, passing out wisdom, deciding disputes, guiding anyone who came to her. Which sounds rather lovely, actually. I'll take a job under a palm tree, just minus the going-to-war bit.

But again, I have questions. Was Deborah the prophet at this time because no men could be found? Or had God uniquely and purposely positioned His daughter to prophesy and judge during such a time as this? As a mother would respond to a child calling out?

King Jabin, his commander Sisera, and their nine hundred iron chariots were no match for the God of Israel, Deborah the prophet, Jael the heroine, and Barak the faithful warrior. God saw all of this coming, and He is the author of our journeys, pen in hand, writing our stories of redemption and restoration and rescue.

Deborah's first move was to summon Barak and to tell him a few things from God. This summoning, if you recall, was a move of authority.[1] Just as King Josiah, as the higher-ranked one, had the right to summon Huldah the prophet to come into his presence (and yet did not), so we can note that Deborah did the summoning and Barak came to her. As the daughter of the Most High King, judge of the Israelites at that time, and prophet to the people, she operated with authority. She knew who God was, she knew who she was, and she served from a secure identity.

And then we see Deborah step into the role of a presidential leader at this moment. McKnight shares the following:

> Deborah was, to use modern analogies, the president, the pope, and Rambo all bundled up in one female body! Judges 4–5 reveals that God called women—it is not mentioned that she is an "exception"—to lead his people. Every reading of her story reveals she was exceptional. . . . To use other terms, she led the nations spiritually, musically, legally, politically, and militarily. Let us not pretend her tasks were social and secular; Deborah was a leader of the entire people of God.[2]

We then see a theme of women at play in this story. The female prophet Deborah gives a word from the Lord to Barak to go, take ten thousand men, and lead them to Mount Tabor. The Lord says He will give Sisera into Barak's hands.

Barak's response to Deborah is this: "If you go with me, I will go; but if you don't go with me, I won't go" (Judges 4:8). Which gives us all the ezer vibes. He's no dummy. He wants a defending ally by his side in war.

Some have thought Barak lacked faith or was cowardly with his response. And it's quite possible. But Ron Pierce gives a more charitable response:

> It is far more likely that Barak wished to have available to him the wisdom and prophetic voice of Deborah while in the uncertainty of battle . . . this was a wise response of a good man to the leadership of an equally good woman.[3]

Regardless of Barak's motive to only go if Deborah came along, Deborah didn't hesitate to join him. But her response to him is quite interesting, as she said, "But because of the course you are taking, the honor will not be yours, for the LORD will deliver Sisera *into the hands of a woman*" (Judges 4:9, emphasis mine). Is the course he is taking a literal or figurative course? Is it the route on land or is it the route of only going with Deborah? Much speculation has risen. But what we do know is that God introduced another woman into the story line who would choose a course of action that would forever change history. And it wasn't Deborah.

———

As Jael worked with her hands that morning, she thought about the hands of the women who had gone before her. They had a strong work ethic; they were worth their salt. As sweat wandered its way down the side of her face, her mind wandered back into the past.

She often thought of her husband's side of the family—of the beautiful, strong, and dark-skinned Zipporah and her industrious way of life. And how Zipporah—what a woman—had married Moses. She had heard so many stories of the famed Moses! Moses, the baby pulled from the Nile, rescued at the hands of a group of women. Moses, who split the Red Sea. Moses, who led the people out of slavery. And Israel was now enslaved again—it had been at least twenty years of oppression under the king of Canaan.

And it wasn't right.

She could feel the battle in her area of the country, the way you feel the oppression of an enemy or the harsh gossip behind your back. She considered her location in this battle. Over time, her husband and his family had moved away from the Israelites and come under the protection of King Jabin and made peace with the oppressor of the Israelites.[4] But an internal battle of justice and righteousness was brewing inside Jael.

It wasn't right.

Jael had heard how King Jabin plundered those he captured, pillaging cities, dividing spoils, a woman or two for each man. She shuddered at the thought of herself being part of the "spoils of war." Of women—image-bearers—being grouped into things. Categorized like weapons, goods, fabric, gold, women.

It wasn't right.

She had also heard that the God of Israel called His people His own treasure. If King Jabin and Commander Sisera plundered the precious treasure of Yahweh, there would be trouble. If the beloved Zipporah, who had gone before her, had worshiped Yahweh, that said something.

And then she saw him. Was that actually Sisera, the commander of the famed chariots of iron? Running . . . away? Away from battle and not toward his men? Where were those shiny newfangled iron chariots now? He was on foot, in the rain, running away from his army. And he was running for her tent.

She had little time to think. Her years of hospitality reflexes taking over, she welcomed the commander right in. Scared, overwhelmed, tired, bloody . . . Sisera looked awful. And awfully thirsty.

He asked for water, for a place to stay, for protection under her roof from his enemy, the Israelites. As Sisera cowardly fled into the house of a woman, the battle inside of Jael ended. She had made her choice.

She made a game-time decision and swapped water with warm milk. This had been a mother's secret sleep weapon for generations. And it would buy her a minute to think. Sisera, with a belly warmed by fresh milk, was fast asleep. She looked around and saw the familiar pegs she had been crafting—pegs that secured tents to the ground. Everyone knows if a tent lacks a third peg, it can no longer stand. Like pride before a fall.

But Jael, Heber's wife, picked up a tent peg and a hammer and went quietly to him while he lay fast asleep, exhausted. She drove the peg through his temple into the ground, and he died.

Just then Barak came by in pursuit of Sisera, and Jael went out to meet him. "Come," she said, "I will show you the man you're looking for." So he went in with her, and there lay Sisera with the tent peg through his temple—dead.

On that day God subdued Jabin king of Canaan before the Israelites. And the hand of the Israelites pressed harder and harder against Jabin king of Canaan until they destroyed him.

Judges 4:21–24

Let it be on record that I am not endorsing the use of a bowl of milk and a tent peg to kill anyone. But let it also be said that in war, the rules are different. When the oppression of God's people is at hand, God brings deliverance. Sometimes God led an entire army into the Red Sea and washed over the enemy chariots until they were defeated. Sometimes a young shepherd boy slayed a menacing giant for victory with one smooth stone and a heart full of faith. Sometimes God worked through a non-Israelite woman, with a few domestic resources in her hands. Sometimes God used a bloody cross with His son on it. But the enemy will always be defeated with God's victorious right hand.

Two women are praised, through song, at the end of it all. Judges 5:24–31 records:

> "Most blessed of women be Jael,
>   the wife of Heber the Kenite,
>   most blessed of tent-dwelling women.

He asked for water, and she gave him milk;
    in a bowl fit for nobles she brought him curdled
      milk.
Her hand reached for the tent peg,
    her right hand for the workman's hammer.
She struck Sisera, she crushed his head,
    she shattered and pierced his temple.
At her feet he sank,
    he fell; there he lay.
At her feet he sank, he fell;
    where he sank, there he fell—dead.
Through the window peered Sisera's mother;
    behind the lattice she cried out,
'Why is his chariot so long in coming?
    Why is the clatter of his chariots delayed?'
The wisest of her ladies answer her;
    indeed, she keeps saying to herself,
'Are they not finding and dividing the spoils:
    a woman or two for each man,
colorful garments as plunder for Sisera,
    colorful garments embroidered,
highly embroidered garments for my neck—
    all this as plunder?'
So may all your enemies perish, Lord!
    But may all who love you be like the sun
      when it rises in its strength."
Then the land had peace forty years.

It's possible Deborah and Jael never even knew one another, but both women are praised as heroines in this valiant song (see all of Judges 5 for Deborah's honor). And not only the heroines, but the voices of women are highlighted in this song. Sisera's own mother has a cameo, wondering where her son could be on his precious chariots and when the men would come home with two women apiece as war plunder?

Turns out two women were warriors, not plunder. Thanks to Deborah and Jael, there would be no such war prize.

Deborah arose as a mother of Israel, responding to the cry of God's people. She led, commanded, and guided Israel to victory. And a big key to unlock the victory? Another woman, Jael. Yes, it's a gruesome narrative and might be hard to stomach—but can we consider the courage it took to take this kind of action? And did you catch what is sung about Jael in Judges 5:24?

> "Most blessed of women be Jael,
>   the wife of Heber the Kenite,
>   most blessed of tent-dwelling women."

This is the same title given to just one other.[5] The mother of God herself, Mary, was also called "blessed among women" (see Luke 1:42). Jael, a woman with courage, ready to crush the enemy with a peg. Mary, a woman of courage, ready to crush the enemy with her son. Both women eyeing the curse in the garden, both women living bravely in the face of a king who oppressed God's people, both blessed among women because of God's purposes and plans.

Dearest daughter, the kingdom of God makes plenty of room for fierce women. Both Deborah and Jael are fierce and faithful fighters. And if you have a fire that rises up inside you for justice and goodness, for a better way in any situation—these are your girls. When you problem-solve quickly and confidently? You are in good company. If you have natural leadership abilities and people look to you for guidance? You stand on Deborah's shoulders. If you look at your resources and use them for justice and righteousness and the kingdom of God? You walk in Jael's wake. Don't let anyone tell you otherwise.

I'm one of the fiery ones. I have been told I am "a lot" with my vision and my voice and my personality over the years. This surprises exactly zero people. I come from a long line of big personalities, loud storytelling, and colorful characters. And I have run some folks over and failed miserably at being gracious in the face of getting things done. In my leadership, I have hurt people and I have made royal messes. I have picked up a tent peg without asking my Father, thinking I needed to slay an enemy when God told me to love her. So, ahem, I am working on it. I need to keep bringing every bit of my personality and my leadership into my Father's hands and let Him shape me. He's the Potter, I'm the clay.

But, friend—even when we have so much to learn as we serve in the kingdom of God—if you have hidden and held back your leadership skills, I invite you to ask God about your gifts. Ask God, *Where and how can I use what you've put in my hands?* Ask Him, and listen. And if you hear nothing? Keep asking, keep listening. He is forming you as you seek Him. And then look for opportunities to serve. Maybe you create your own ways, or you walk in a way someone has opened up for you. God hasn't given you your unique set of gifts to be hidden. He has given His daughters gifts of leadership for His glory and our good.

The scene ends with the final word of the True Victor. To God be the glory, the winner of our battles: "On that day *God* subdued Jabin king of Canaan before the Israelites" (Judges 4:23, emphasis mine).

May this verse bring us a kind and gentle reminder as the stories unfold. God was the true Hero, putting women in place to bring about His redemptive purposes. May we not forget He is the Hero, the only one worthy of our worship. Even as women are highlighted in the early chapters of Judges, God is the one to be worshiped. Even as we uncover the unsung women of the Bible, may we never worship them. May we honor them, stand upon their shoulders, learn from them, and walk in their brave shoes. But our worship, our adoration, our lives—the God who saves is the only one worthy of those.

8

The Immigrant

We Are Fully Welcomed

No Ammonite or Moabite or any of their descendants
may enter the assembly of the Lord, not even in the tenth
generation.

Deuteronomy 23:3[1]

Though Deborah judged and peace reigned under her leadership, Israel turned aside and worshiped other gods again afterward. They lost sight of the leadership of the mother of Israel, and much greater, they lost sight of the Almighty God, who provided everything for them.

A famine hit, and faith was as scarce as food.

And true to who we know our Creator God to be, who wrangles chaos into order, mayhem into shalom, darkness into day, God—in the darkest of days—sheds light. In the darkest of days, God's heart is stirred with compassion. In the darkest of days, God gives us a story of a woman.

God gives us Ruth.

Ruth is a light in a dark nation. However, Ruth is from a nation God had said to stay away from. God had called the Israelites not to do business with, to worship with, or to live with Ruth's kind. Why? Because she hailed from enemy camp—the Moabites—a nation that had horrific worship practices, including child sacrifice. And God loves His children fiercely.

And yet God, in His compassion and grace, widens the table. Over time we see God welcome even the worst nations to worship Him, if they choose. The invitational heart of God never tires of passing out invites. His plan all along was to make a family through Abraham, who would then, in turn, widen the table to bless *all* the families of the earth. Every last one of them. God's heart cries out, sometimes audibly through the prophets, for all to come.

> Come, take your choice of wine or milk—it's all free! . . . Come to me with your ears wide open. Listen, and you will find life. . . . Let the wicked change their ways and banish the very thought of doing wrong. Let them turn to the Lord that he may have mercy on them. Yes, turn to our God, for he will forgive generously.
>
> Isaiah 55:1, 3, 7 NLT

A daughter, Ruth the Moabite, shows us the way.

If you have ever felt like you're in survival mode and you're fighting some serious bitterness, you are not alone. When it's hit after hit in life, and there doesn't seem like any light is at the end of this long, lonely tunnel. The medical bills are relentless. The car won't start. Your husband is cold. Your teen is spiraling into depression, again. The weight of the world is on your shoulders, and it's a daily battle to get out of bed. You can't fix it.

God has included many stories about women for many reasons. One of those reasons is so we don't feel alone, and we can see ourselves in this story. Let yourself walk in Naomi's shoes for a few minutes. Feel what she feels. And watch her God provide.

Survival. This was the word that had lodged itself in the back of her throat. They moved away from their hometown of Bethlehem—the House of Bread[2]—because there was no longer any bread to be found. A famine had reached their land, and they needed to find food. The goal was survival.

Then, after this painful move away from a place she knew like the back of her hand—*her home*—Naomi's husband died and her sons passed away. Bitterness was her home, survival was her wallpaper, loneliness was her food.

News had traveled through Moab that the Lord had blessed His people with good crops again. Could her empty soul find fullness again? Was going home the best option? Would she ever know what it was to have a full table, with wine and bread and olives overflowing again? Questions swirled in her mind night after night as she considered the long trek home. She was sleepless and restless, tossing and turning about staying or going.

Finally, she decided. She would go. She would return home. But bitterness had gotten the best of her, rooting itself deep inside her chest. She would return home, but she would still go empty-handed and hard-hearted.

The three women bound by the same last name stood there, too long, saying their goodbyes to those they loved. Naomi's daughters-in-law were coming, leaving behind their own mothers. Tearful goodbyes, promises to visit soon, sesame bread pressed into palms for the journey, one last hug to send them on their way. The two daughters-in-law were leaving behind the long-standing Moabite recipes, orally passed on in kitchens so the next generation could memorize the lentil stews and the savory sauces. They were leaving behind the rhythm of Sunday dinners. They were leaving behind their grandmother's hands. The hands that helped and cooked and cleaned and worked alongside their daughters and their daughters' daughters. They were leaving behind huge parts of their hearts. But still, Orpah and Ruth had married Naomi's sons—now passed—and committed to Naomi and her family. They were committed to Ruth. So to Judah they went.

As they followed the winding road, swirls of dust kicking up, her thoughts kicked up with them. The farther they walked, the further into her feelings Naomi went. *Why are my daughters-in-law coming with me? What do I have to offer them? Could I still give birth to two more sons, and then they'd grow all the way up, and then they'd marry Orpah and Ruth? Don't be ridiculous, that's far too long. And besides, I'm too old to even get married again. Who would want me? Who is my age and even still alive, let alone alive and single?* All of this was absurd. She stopped and swiveled around, looking at her daughters-in-law square in the face.

"Girls. Turn around. Go back home. This is a fool's errand. May the Lord reward you for your kindness to your husband and to me. May He bless you with the security of another marriage. Return to your own mothers and your own people and your own land."

Shocked, the girls dropped their sacks and stared at Naomi. And then the tears came. Relief mingled with disbelief, commitment tangled up with fear. They wept, hugged, and wept more. They wept for the loss of their husbands. They had bonded through grief, each of them knowing the depth of loss. The depth of fear and insecurity and no sons to hold. They wept for the struggle of survival. They wept for being single in their culture. They wept because they had stuck together, but this reality was pulling them apart. What should the daughters do? What choice should they make? To be at home with their husbands' mother, or home with their own? It was too much to bear.

What seemed like hours later, Orpah kissed her mother-in-law goodbye. She sighed, looked up to the heavens, and chose to go home. But Ruth was different. Ruth clung tightly to Naomi, whispering covenant-like words:

> "Don't ask me to leave you and turn back. Wherever you go, I will go; wherever you live, I will live. Your people will be my people, and your God will be my God. Wherever you die, I will die, and there I will be buried. May the LORD punish me severely if I allow anything but death to separate us!" When Naomi saw that Ruth was determined to go with her, she said nothing more.
>
> Ruth 1:16–18 NLT

Word spreads fast in small-town Israel. As soon as the town came into focus, a crowd of folks greeted Naomi and Ruth and they brimmed with joy and excitement. The town she had built her life around had not forgotten her and was welcoming her with open, compassionate arms.

But Naomi crossed her arms instead. When they shouted, "Naomi! It's you!" she replied with a bitter plea.

> "Don't call me Naomi," she responded. "Instead, call me Mara, for the Almighty has made life very bitter for me. I went away full, but the Lord has brought me home empty. Why call me Naomi when the Lord has caused me to suffer and the Almighty has sent such tragedy upon me?" So Naomi returned from Moab, accompanied by her daughter-in-law

Ruth, the young Moabite woman. They arrived in Bethlehem in late spring, at the beginning of the barley harvest.

Ruth 1:20–22 NLT

———

There have been many places where I felt like I did not belong. Where there were clearly established rules and I didn't fit them. No one felt warm or welcoming, and everything in me wanted to run right out of there as fast as possible. My body was saying "get up and go" but my mind was saying "stay and be brave," and the internal conflict was strong. *Does God want me here? Or can I leave? Is He doing something, and I am part of it? Or am I free to walk out of here? How long should I stay? Hours? Days? Months? Years?* A daughter's heart is a complex place.

Friend, if you have felt your mind go one way and your body go another in a space where you didn't belong, me too. And so did Ruth. She knew what it was to be pushed to the edges of a room, internally conflicted. I am sure she was on high alert and endured microaggressions and side-eyes. Whether discrimination is subtle or overt, it's real and it's maddening. If you have been a foreigner in any measure, you feel the gap between belonging and beloved. And it's a lonely space.

If you are in that space right now, would you allow yourself the gift of a slow inhale and a long exhale, right this moment? And as you exhale, let Ruth minister to those painful moments you are holding in your body. Find yourself in this important story. See how God is tilling some of the hardest fields, how He cares for you when the ground is dry and cracked and you feel alone.

Ruth had a social-emotional awareness about her. She saw how some looked at her with disdain because a Moabite had moved into town. She heard how some of the Israelite women whispered about her, the foreigner. But some of the women were kind to her; some women knew all too well their own emptiness and their own poverty and reached out in solidarity. Upon their arrival, one woman took Ruth's hands in hers and shared how the Lord saw them and would provide for them. This older, kind woman passed on the words from the Israelite law that had saved her life years ago:

> When you are harvesting your crops and forget to bring in a bundle of grain from your field, don't go back to get it. Leave it for the foreigners, orphans, and widows. Then the LORD your God will bless you in all you do.
>
> Deuteronomy 24:19 NLT

So Ruth set out to the fields to see if she could gather what had been dropped for her, the foreigner. Maybe she could gather up a blessing. Hopefully the owner of the field she picked would remember the old law and have mercy on her, a foreigner.

———

As I have been highlighting God's daughters and His overwhelming love for you and me, I don't want to miss God's sons in the story. Especially the ones who reflected His heart of compassion, who saw a need and moved toward it, like a mother protecting her chicks.

I have several brothers in my life who have cleared a path, used their privilege, seen the need, and have responded with care, concern, and compassion. Maybe it was an uncle for you. Or a grandfather. Or a coworker. Or a neighbor. But if a man (or several) has come to mind who has been an absolute gift to you, these are the Boazes we can thank God for and sing a song of thanksgiving about. Boaz gives us a beautiful picture of a man after God's own heart, a son of the Most High King.

Boaz had been away in a neighboring town and was looking forward to getting home. As he rounded the street corner and headed home, his fields came into view and he greeted his harvesters with the blessing he always said upon them, because he believed it to be true.

"The LORD be with you!" he said.

"The LORD bless you!" the harvesters replied (Ruth 2:4 NLT).

Knowing Boaz to be an upright man, they heartily blessed him back.

And then Boaz saw her.

Who was that young woman also working hard, gathering grain? He hadn't ever seen her before, but his heart swelled with compassion. And maybe a bit of attraction. She clearly worked hard, but she also kept her distance.

> Boaz went over and said to Ruth, "Listen, my daughter. Stay right here with us when you gather grain; don't go to any other fields. Stay right behind the young women working in my field. See which part of the field they are harvesting, and then follow them. I have warned the young men not to treat you roughly. And when you are thirsty, help yourself to the water they have drawn from the well."
>
> Ruth fell at his feet and thanked him warmly. "What have I done to deserve such kindness?" she asked. "I am only a foreigner."
>
> "Yes, I know," Boaz replied. "But I also know about everything you have done for your mother-in-law since the death of your husband. I have heard how you left your father and mother and your own land to live here among complete strangers. May the LORD, the God of

Israel, under whose wings you have come to take refuge, reward you fully for what you have done."

Ruth 2:8–12 NLT

Ruth stumbled back, ever so slightly, at his kindness. And at his blessing. Boaz declared that she had come under the wings of God, like a baby chick protected under the wings of her mother. God was mothering her, in the wake of having left her own mother. The compassion of God was striking to her. And, so were Boaz's biceps.

"Boaz's field? You could *not* have picked a better field!" Naomi exclaimed. "He will make sure you're protected, not harassed. He's known for his generosity. Did he offer you lunch at mealtime? Of course he did! Stay with his field all summer long. What a gift to have him looking out for you!" Naomi, grateful for their good fortune, slept well for the first time in weeks.

She had always trusted Naomi; it was part of why she came back to Naomi's world. Her wisdom was unparalleled in most situations, and this was no exception. Ruth would do everything Naomi suggested to do, though some of it was a bit odd.

Ruth understood taking a bath, washing her hair, using lovely perfume, looking good. That always helped with signaling she would be a good catch.

But the part where she was supposed to uncover Boaz's feet and lie down by them? Maybe it was an old wives' tale of Israel custom that had worked in the past? What if his feet smelled . . . and she couldn't take it? How long was she supposed to stay there? What if she startled him and he was angered and didn't allow her to come back into his fields to glean? What was she getting herself into?

Her mind kept running away with crazy thoughts. Breathing, she calmed herself by coaching her soul. Either way, Boaz was nothing but kind, and she had acted only in good standing and excellence. If he mistook this gesture, her record would speak for her.

"Tell me everything, my daughter!" Naomi said.

"He told me not to worry about a thing, and that everyone in town knows I am a woman of excellence! Which is huge, Naomi, because I am a foreigner! But it does, in fact, seem God has spread His wings over me and brought protection and provision. He also said just what you said—he is a kinsman redeemer. But he's not the closest one who could marry me and redeem our family. He knows of one other guy even closer, and he has to talk it over with him first. But if that guy is not willing, he certainly is!"

After Ruth told Naomi everything Boaz had said to her, she added, "He gave me these six scoops of barley and said, 'Don't go back to your mother-in-law empty-handed.'"

Empty-handed. That had been Naomi's bitter song for so long. And maybe that has been yours, too. Where you once held dreams, you hold disappointment. What you imagined your life to be isn't anything like what you have right now. Naomi knows. And God sees. And He sees your empty hands. So may I, with all compassion, suggest your empty hands are something God has plans to fill? He is a God of abundance. He is a God who owns the cattle on a thousand hills (see Psalm 50:10–12). He is a God who has not forgotten you. He knows the dreams buried deep in your heart. And He has scoops of grace upon grace for your hands. His goodness and mercy are chasing after you (see Psalm 23:6). He knows and He sees and He has gifts for you. He is working as you are waiting. And He is never late. Watch Naomi.

Before Ruth left, Boaz sent six scoops of barley with her. A gift just for Naomi. A reminder that God saw her, God noticed her need, God was with her. Naomi's mind went back to creation, to the number of days of work when the world was created, and then the day of rest after those six. Could six scoops of barley signal a day of rest was coming?[3] Could she truly rest in God's provision now? Would God redeem her bitterness and name her blessed?

If you feel like Naomi, ask God for six scoops of barley. Open your hands to humbly receive His gifts. Or, I say this with all tenderness, ask Him to help you see the scoops He has already given you. Scoops of forgiveness. Scoops removing shame and then clothing you with His love. Scoops of healing you have forgotten about. Scoops of peace where there should have been anxiety. Scoops of His provision when there was no other way.

———

Boaz followed the law in every way possible. He went straight to the city gates to find the relative who was first in line to buy Naomi's property—which also meant marrying Ruth and giving her a son to carry on Naomi's line.

After a good chat at the city gates, the other man said he couldn't do it. He had property of his own to take care of, and this new situation would jeopardize his own inheritance. Which left Boaz the opportunity to redeem the property, marry Ruth, and continue the lineage of Naomi and Elimelech.

So they swapped sandals, like you do, to seal the deal. The first handshake was a sandal shake. (Did they give them back? Was it for keeps? Did they now have to live with mismatched shoes? What about sizes? How stinky was this endeavor?)

Apparently, when transferring a right of purchase, sandals were removed and handed to the other party. And no sandals have ever been sweeter than the sandals exchanged that day.

On that day, daughters were blessed. Daughters were given protection, provision, blessing, honor, and restoration. Naomi and Ruth were seen, heard, and loved. And so are you. Because of them.

When Boaz purchased Naomi's land, Ruth was a big part of the deal. An Israelite would marry a Moabite, which was ripe ground for objection and outrage, as Ruth hailed from the land that had been banned from coming into the Israelite assembly.

But God had different plans, and those plans included his daughters. Even the ones outside of Israel—the foreigners, the outcasts. God not only included Ruth but welcomed her in with lavish generosity. God had planned all along to bring a bounty in the middle of a famine by way of forbidden fruit.

A Moabite, of all women, was going to be right in the middle of the redemption of Israel. Right in the lineage of the greatest Son to ever grace the earth. Ruth was emphatically blessed by the elders and all the folks at the city gate that day!

And as they blessed her, they wished her offspring like those of Rachel and Leah. They wished her sons in the line of Judah, the tribe from which King David himself would eventually come. And the Messiah Himself.

And that is exactly what happened. God's table extended to a nation that had been cut off. His compassionate love is full of kindness and generosity. God's imagination made a blessing out of an oxymoron: a virtuous Moabite. God saw Naomi, God saw Ruth, and God saw fit to bless Ruth's lineage with the King of Kings and the Lord of Lords.

The book ends with the genealogical record of her son, Obed, who would become the grandfather of David. The great-great-great-grandfather of Jesus.

The book named *Ruth* is a story of light in the darkness.

Ruth, a foreigner, outside the Israelites.

Ruth, a light in the dark days of the judges.

Ruth, a loyal and faithful woman to her mother-in-law, a resourceful and determined woman to her husband.

Because of Ruth, we have a Redeemer.

Because of Ruth, we have a Savior.

Because of Ruth, we have Jesus.

HEALING

This section is about healing. About the bravery to open yourself up to the Father and to show Him your wounds. This is about finding safety where there has been fear and rejection. About finding compassion where you have seen condemnation. About finding integration and wholeness in places where there has been disintegration and fracturing.

You, dearest daughter, are making your way into your Father's arms. He longs to wrap His strength around you and tell you that it's okay. He's here. You are safe. You are secure. You will not be betrayed. You will be taken care of. You are home in Him.

9

The Forgotten

We Are Remembered

In her deep anguish Hannah prayed to the Lord, weeping
bitterly.

1 Samuel 1:10

This is a tender one. I've been here. Crying out to God,
asking for a baby. Wondering if it's me. Questioning what
I could do differently. Sparring with some self-deprecating
thoughts that are more stealthy than a ninja in a dark alley.
Hannah is a woman God has given us so we can leave our
shame behind about our tears. She is here to lead us spiritually and emotionally. She shows us what it means to un-
ashamedly ask God for what she wants. She reminds us we
are remembered.

God is disappointed in you, that's why. That's why God isn't answering your prayers. That's why this is happening to you. This is your fault.

Hannah's self-talk was spiraling. Again. The cocktail of self-pity and grief coated with a salty rim of anxiety sat in front of her, begging her to indulge.

Why has God chosen to open that woman's womb and not mine?

Why does God seem to pour favor on some but not others?

Why am I harassed day after day by her?

Does God even see me?

Why do I feel so forgotten?

Where is God in this—isn't the command to be fruitful and multiply? I am trying!

There was nothing she could do to make herself pregnant. She had no control of her body's ability to create a baby. She was out of answers, out of her own strength, out of herself. The very thing she wanted so desperately was desperately out of reach. And though her friends were well-meaning, no amount of herbs or diets they suggested were changing anything.

And Peninnah, her husband's other wife? She was the absolute worst. All she did was taunt her. Mean-spirited and cutting, her words just added salt to Hannah's wound. And she only said nasty things when Elkanah, their husband, wasn't around. He would walk back into the room, and Peninnah would be sweet as pie, like nothing happened. Even though she had just cut Hannah down to size, bringing tears to her eyes. She was a thorn in her side. Gaslighting at its finest.

Elkanah was so sweet, so kind. *Please eat, My Love,* he would say to Hannah. *Why are you so depressed? You have me! Aren't I better than ten sons?*

He would never understand. Her heart's cry ran deep, and she was slowly drowning in her sorrow.

One night she had had enough. She resolutely stood up after dinner, quietly cleared her plate, marched straight to the Tabernacle, and flopped on her knees. And wept. The kind of weeping where your snot drips down your face, your body shakes, your dignity is long gone. Her tears were traveling the same road the unloved Leah traveled. Leah—the rejected, the unseen, the forgotten.

Utterly alone, the floodgates finally opened. Her grief, her lament, her request were like a waterfall pouring over the side of a cliff. She dumped every plea she could find inside her heart to Yahweh. He is the great I AM. If anyone would understand, it would be the one who has womb-like compassion.

Is she drunk? Seriously? She should be embarrassed by her behavior—she looks ridiculous! Eli the priest watched Hannah's lips moving, but no sound came out.

What was this nonsense? This woman dared darken the door of the house of God with this behavior?

"Must you come here drunk? Throw away your wine!" Eli demanded.

He startled her. *How long had the priest been there? And did he just ask her if she was drunk? Oh for the love. Maybe drunk on grief? Does that work?*

"Oh no, sir!" she replied. "I haven't been drinking wine or anything stronger. But I am very discouraged, and I was pouring out my heart to the Lord. Don't think I am a wicked woman! For I have been praying out of great anguish and sorrow."

1 Samuel 1:15–16 NLT

I was pouring my heart out to the Lord.

Before any psalmist had the words for such a gesture, Hannah showed us how. Scripture freezes this moment in time for us, a time capsule of how to honor our bodies as women. The pages hold her anguish and despair, displaying what it means to be in God's presence in our pain. It is a pouring. A spilling out of everything that has come to the surface, flowing into a safe space. It is an embodiment of lament. And then of healing. And it was the only thing left to do. To take her heart, like a fragile glass pitcher, and slowly let every desire and ache cascade out of her, letting them tumble into her Father's hands. So often we, as women, stuff our feelings. We bury them, ignore them, and put a stiff hand up to them, telling them they aren't welcome here. Our emotional stuffing is slowly deteriorating our souls. But Hannah honored her feelings, her desires, her wants. She let them come up and over and out before the safest place she could think of—her compassionate God.

Hannah teaches us how to pour out our heart, how to hold pain, and how to heal, and her example was a cue King David picked up in his psalm-writing later on: "Trust in him at all times, you people; pour out your hearts to him, for God is our refuge" (Psalm 62:8). The great writer and worshiper, the man after God's own heart, pointed back to the words of a weepy, barren woman. King David colors in the page from Hannah's initial outline. He tells us it is God alone who can be trusted with our heart's treasures. He alone can handle the pouring, can hold every drop, can be our refuge. No other friend can hold the depths of our heart. And the Father's hands are kind, compassionate, and good. He treats our tears with tenderness, bottles them as precious oil, and gives us Hannah to be our guide.

After Eli's eyes adjusted to Hannah's pouring out—something he hadn't seen before—a blessing bubbled to the surface for her.

Eli answered, "Go in peace, and may the God of Israel grant you what you have asked of him." She said, "May your servant find favor in your eyes." Then she went her way and ate something, and her face was no longer downcast.

1 Samuel 1:17–18

Hannah, in her pouring out, had asked to be remembered. In her tears, she asked God to not forget her, to give her a son, one she would dedicate to God's service. It's like Hannah read my mail. And I'm grateful.

Again, Scripture slows down to zoom in on Hannah's heart. And her heart reveals our heart. She displays one of our deepest fears: that we would be forgotten. That we would be overlooked, passed by, invisible. So often we feel that invisibility. We feel erased in the room, in the narrative, in the system. Maybe we feel we are too much, too single, too dark, too light, too heavy, too loud, too honest, too playful, too questioning, too odd, too ambitious, too different, too creative, too weird, too quiet. Being invisible is a deep fear of so many daughters.

So can God forget you? Is that real? Can He erase you from His memory and move on?

No way, Daughters. God cannot forget you. If God is God, He cannot forget you. He is omniscient, knowing everything—He knows the past, present, future. To forget would be contrary to God's character. He cannot possibly forget.

Hannah's story helps us wrestle our question to the very bottom of the pit of our fear. Her story makes us search out the very real possibility of being forgotten. And when we do the necessary digging, we understand what the writer was saying about the idea of God *remembering*. The key is this: When God remembers, He takes action. The Hebrew word *zakar* is to remember, and we see God remembering Noah in Genesis 8:1 as a wind was sent and the waters receded. God took action. Just as the Israelites were told to "remember the Sabbath day, to keep it holy" (Exodus 20:8 ESV), so they were to observe it, to follow the instructions. To take action. "In each passage that says, 'God remembered,' we see that the phrase is followed by some sort of action or work on behalf of God's people."[1] Times God acted, intervened, rescued.

And just as God says He will remember our sins no more (Jeremiah 31:34, Hebrews 8:12, Hebrews 10:17), this means He will not act against our sins anymore, as justice was served through Jesus as the final act of atonement.

When God remembered Hannah, He took action and opened her womb.

Never once will God forget a daughter. And never once will He forget about *you*. He will not have amnesia toward you, a soul He was so delighted to form. As we read in Psalm 139, He knows when you sit and when you rise. He knows your thoughts (and loves you no matter what they are!). He knows your coming and going. He knows even the very hairs on your head, as Luke 12:7 says.

The gift Hannah has given us is her honesty to ask the question, the courage to pour out her pain, and the openness to receive the reward of a God who acts on behalf of His people. A God who sees, hears, feels, and is moved. A God who knows the depths of your soul as you seek to pour it out before Him. He is a God of compassion, moving toward you with empathy and power.

She felt a revival in her bones. When Eli prophesied that God would bless her request, Hannah got up, ate something, and her spirit was much lighter. This deep moment of pouring out had poured into her faith. With a pouring comes a healing. She came in with despair and left with hope. She emptied herself, and God filled her with blessing. And by faith, she made love to her husband.

She had hardly ever linked faith to lovemaking, but maybe it was time to start. How else was God going to fulfill her request if she didn't also walk by faith? As God remembered—moved into action—toward Hannah, Hannah also took a step of faith toward her husband. This all felt so risky, but also so hopeful. She had often separated the sacred and the secular, but here—in this moment—she knew all of life was spiritual. She was trusting God in her bedroom, of all places. But if she was going to believe God, she was going to have to take that to the bank.

Elkanah made love to his wife Hannah, and the LORD remembered her. So in the course of time Hannah became pregnant and gave birth to a son. She named him Samuel, saying, "Because I asked the LORD for him."

1 Samuel 1:19–20

Because she asked the Lord for him.

This is for those who ask. For those who keep asking. And for those who just haven't asked yet. For the daughters who wonder if asking will open up a door that they will never be able to shut because the flood of emotion and possibility and fear will overwhelm them. Hannah poured out her heart, and God took action. Hannah walked by faith right into her bedroom, and God blessed her. Hannah asked God, and God gave graciously.

But Hannah's asking might make us ask another question. Is it my faith that causes God to give me what I have in my heart? And if I don't have enough faith, then is that why I don't have what I am hoping for? And here we run into the mysterious complexity of an awesome God. Hannah's faith is indeed stunning. Before the writer of Hebrews penned it, she showed us how to boldly "approach God's throne of grace with confidence, so that we may receive mercy and find grace to help us in our time of need" (Hebrews 4:16).

But we know God is not a cosmic genie, granting us our every wish. We do know that God is a faithful God who keeps His word to the covenant He made with Abraham. And He will keep it. God remembered—acted upon—His covenant with His people through Hannah. God acted because of His covenant to His people, because of His faithfulness to a faithless nation, and because of His compassionate love toward a rebellious people. He had a great covenant to fulfill, as He said He would. So God gave Hannah a son, Samuel, who then later anointed David king. Because God has a redemptive plan for the whole of history. And Hannah's tears are involved in this redemptive work. It is then through the line of David that God's covenant was fulfilled in the life, death, and resurrection of Jesus.

And Hannah's response? She sings like a hummingbird. She sings a song foreshadowing Mary's song in so many beautiful ways. A song that points to who God is: a sovereign Rock, a just God, a mighty King who feeds the hungry, lifts the needy, who gives and takes away, who gives barren women children. She sings a song to God and about God as she dedicates and then leaves her son in the house of God. From being taunted by Peninnah to pouring out her soul to making love by faith to dedicating her precious son—Hannah fought to focus her eyes back on God.

Hannah doesn't show us how to be perfect; she shows us how to be human. Hannah shows us how to mourn, how to weep, how to pour out, how to receive, how to trust, how to lay our most precious treasure down, how to sing.

So much grace and mercy abounded all before the great prophet Samuel entered the story. Samuel, the one who would hear the voice of God, in a time when hearing was rare. Samuel, who would hear God tell him the brother he was looking for was not lined up but out being a shepherd. Samuel, the one who would pour oil over David to one day be king. Before there was Samuel, there was a mother who poured, who prayed, who wept, who stayed, who was blessed, who believed God in every kind of way.

I have had long seasons of pouring out my heart like Hannah, asking for something to change. But it was the waiting, the asking, the begging, the praying that changed me. When you pour out your heart like Hannah, you are stepping into a river that will change you forever. Your pouring, like Hannah's, is part of a process you don't want to pass up. I don't love long processes. I am partial to quick answers and speedy solutions. I have always talked fast and walked fast. I like speed. So I have had to practice slowing down long enough to name my emotions and lay them all out before God. But I am practicing, and little by little, God is forming me in the pouring.

Your pouring, weeping, praying, waiting, asking . . . these are forming you into a daughter who trusts God. Which is gold, sister. You will be a daughter who looks back at the pouring out of your soul and sees how your growth, your resolve, your character, and your friendship with your Father are stronger than they were before you started pouring out everything. Take courage. Hannah is good company.

10

The Nameless

We Are Important

> At this time Aramean raiders had invaded the land of Israel,
> and among their captives was a young girl who had been
> given to Naaman's wife as a maid.
>
> 2 Kings 5:2 NLT

He had us turn to Second Kings, chapter five in class. Professor Don Payne, the kindest, most thoughtful, most pastoral seminary professor I had encountered, took us to a passage I was not very familiar with. I didn't grow up reading Bible stories, and I had to work hard to physically find this story in my Bible, trying not to look like the girl who cannot name all sixty-six books of the Bible by heart. Even though it's true. I didn't grow up singing Bible songs or with felt boards or any of the other tales I've heard about when it comes to Sunday school. I opened my first Bible at sixteen, and it felt like a wild place. Because it is.

Dr. Payne always made space for our questions, our observations, our tears as we read the text together. And this story was no exception. This one includes a girl who was kidnapped, taken from her family, and enslaved. And then she did the unthinkable.

She combed her oppressor's thick, gorgeous hair. The wife of her master was in her care as she carefully worked through the tangles of the woman's almond-colored mane. It was her favorite time of day, the post-bath routine. The rich olive oil candles burned, and pomegranate perfume was sprayed. Assigned to Namaan's wife, the young girl had been abruptly removed from her home, her family, her culture, and then tasked to serve in a foreigner's house. Overnight she went from free to enslaved. From dreaming about the Hebrew boy next door to scrubbing the floors of her oppressor. If she let herself cry at all, the floodgates would never close. So she didn't.

She willed herself to seek out small moments in her day to concentrate on a tactile job in front of her. When she worked with her hands, she could distract the ache of her heart. The ache of not being with her own mother. The ache of her lost future. The ache of being captured and contained, like a caged kingfisher sentenced to never fly again.

Combing her master's wife's hair was something she would have done with her sisters' long locks back home, so she chose to enjoy it. And something happens when women get together and talk hair, makeup, and beauty. The crown of their head is the gateway to the crevice of their heart. Soon enough, Namaan's servant and his wife found themselves braided together as they shared hair secrets, recipes, remedies, gossip, news, and stories.

On one of these evenings, after Namaan's wife had bathed, the girl from the land of Israel sensed a heavy heart. What was troubling her master's wife? Why the deep exhales tonight?

She shared with the girl that Namaan's skin disease was becoming worse, and she was frightened at how the disease was slowly taking over. He had recently slammed his toe in the door but kept working, not knowing that he had left a trail of blood throughout the house. How long had he been bleeding? How much blood had been lost? These moments were becoming more and more frequent. His lack of pain was not a gift—it was a curse. Concern and anxiety for her husband was written all over her face.

"I wish my master would go to see the prophet in Samaria. He would heal him of his leprosy," offered the young girl. She knew of Elisha. She knew the God of Israel. And she knew God could heal.

Namaan's wife's eyes lit up. She would try anything. That night, Namaan's wife suggested this to him. Just as desperate as she was, Namaan took her advice. And soon Namaan made some arrangements. He gathered 750 pounds of silver, 150 pounds of gold, and ten sets of clothing. He drafted a letter to go ahead of him. Armed with his power, his prestige, and his pride, Namaan was ready to buy back his health and get his healing.

The girl from the land of Israel. That's all that is recorded of her name. We are given no history. No details. No family name. Nothing else. A young girl had been taken captive and given to Namaan's wife as a maid. She was enslaved. But she still had a voice. David Guzik writes, "This young girl was an outstanding example of a faithful witness in her current circumstance. She *cared* enough to speak up, and she had *faith* enough to believe that Elisha would heal him of his leprosy."[1] She had compassion on her oppressor. If only we could be as godly as this little girl.

So Namaan, the powerful warrior, trusted the powerless, nameless girl from the land of Israel. More than one script was about to be flipped.

And maybe, dearest daughter, it's your script that must be flipped. Maybe you feel unseen and unnamed in your season. Or quite possibly for most of your life. You have felt under-utilized, undervalued, underrated. Or you've seen those with more privilege, position, and power unjustly chosen over you. You are not alone.

We may not know the girl from the land of Israel's name, but God does. God sees her, God knows her, and God calls her daughter. When you find yourself entering a new space, a new job, or a new neighborhood and no one knows your name or story yet, take a moment to remember who always knows. Your Father. You and your Father know, and that is an intimate thing. That is a sweet little secret you have between the two of you. Being privately known in the face of public obscurity might be the gift you need so that you linger in your Father's arms. He loves when we linger.

There have been some settings where I've tried to practice obscurity. Where I only share a few things and I don't try to win the moment with a title. I'll have you know, I would much rather win you over with a name like *author* and take the spotlight than to be hidden. But sometimes God whispers to my soul, "I see you." And that is enough. In those moments it's good for me to be obscure, to be hidden in my Father's arms.

The girl from the land of Israel is going to be one of the first I find in heaven to ask her name and hold it with honor. I admire her. She took great risks and did great things. Whether the world knew her name or not.

———

Namaan seemed to really think it was about power, money, and status when it came to healing. So Namaan, the Syrian, a Gentile outside of the blessing of God's people, would take his money (estimated at "more than $1.2 million," showing "how *desperate* Naaman's condition was"[2]) and go straight to his boss, the king of Aram. And after a discussion, the king of Aram sent word to the king of Israel on behalf of Namaan, the brave and valiant warrior.

But the king of Israel was outraged by this request. He wanted nothing to do with this nonsense. Someone from Syria was coming to him for healing? How ridiculous. He wasn't in charge of healing and he didn't have that kind of power and they were not friends with Syria. Was this a trick? A trap? Was he looking to start a war? Why was Namaan being sent from the king of Aram to him?

But Elisha the prophet caught wind that a mighty warrior from Syria had come seeking healing. And he told King Jehoram to chill. Have Namaan come to Elijah. He would take care of it.

So Namaan, along with his horse, chariots, money, and pride, headed to Elisha's house. But Elisha himself didn't come out. He sent a messenger. Slice one of humble pie was served. Elisha didn't give him the honor of greeting him personally. And Namaan wasn't having it.

> But Naaman went away angry and said, "I thought that he would surely come out to me and stand and call on the name of the LORD his God, wave his hand over the spot and cure me of my leprosy. Are not Abana and Pharpar, the rivers of Damascus, better than all the waters of Israel? Couldn't I wash in them and be cleansed?" So he turned and went off in a rage.
>
> 2 Kings 5:11–12

We can almost see the smoke coming out of Namaan's very significant ears: *Where is my parade? Where is my very newsworthy light show of healing? I thought Elisha would wave magical hands over my body. Where is Elisha himself?*

And after a humble, nameless servant girl from Israel had interceded for Namaan's healing, more servants interceded. The bravery of the subordinates in this situation is significant.[3] Namaan's servants, who had heard the instructions from Elisha's messenger, saw Namaan's prideful reaction and decided to pull Namaan aside and give him the truth.

The servants told him, "This is not hard, Namaan. He said to wash and be clean. He could have asked you to do so many harder, bigger, grander things. Just take a bath, man. Not hard. Just do it."

God never ceases to use the weak to shame the strong. It's always Opposite Day in the kingdom of God. Where daughters point to the healing power of God in the face of the oppressing power of evil. Where subordinates give advice to their superiors. Where the proud are humbled, and healing is still available even if anger and pride came first. Where a bath in a river is the best thing you can do. Where repentance can always change a life.

And Namaan repented.

He went down to the Jordan (all the John and Jesus in the Jordan baptism vibes), dipped himself seven times, according to what Elisha instructed, "and his flesh was restored like the flesh of a little child, and he was clean" (2 Kings 5:14 ESV).

Like the youthful flesh of a little girl, some might say. He took on the childlike posture of the girl who started this whole journey. He had to become like the nameless, humble girl to encounter the living, healing God.

Namaan had a certain expectation of how things ought to work. But God gives grace to the humble. To the ones who say, "This is about Your will, Your way, Your power, Your kingdom. Not mine."

And not only was his skin healed but so was his heart. Namaan, a Syrian, outside of the people of Israel, became a believer in the Most High God.

> Then Naaman and all his attendants went back to the man of God. He stood before him and said, "Now I know that there is no God in all the world except in Israel. So please accept a gift from your servant."
>
> 2 Kings 5:15

This time, Namaan's offer of a gift was about gratitude for his healing, not about earning his healing with his money. His heart was changed, and he testified to the God who heals lepers.

God's power and grace are in the middle of this moment. And the girl from Israel points the way.

For the daughter who wonders about her lack of power, prestige, and position: Yours is the kingdom of heaven. Humility is prized in the kingdom of God, starting with children. And this young girl takes our hand and leads the way. Enslaved and captive, she still points to the One who frees and heals. We know nothing more of her after this. Was she freed for her wisdom? Was she positioned to a great place of service, like Jospeh because of his dreams? What is the rest of her story?

We see Jesus speak of this moment centuries later—of how this young girl ushered in a widening of the table once again. A Gentile was healed because a young girl testified about Elisha.

> "Truly I tell you," he continued, "no prophet is accepted in his hometown. I assure you that there were many widows in

Israel in Elijah's time, when the sky was shut for three and a half years and there was a severe famine throughout the land. Yet Elijah was not sent to any of them, but to a widow in Zarephath in the region of Sidon. And there were many in Israel with leprosy in the time of Elisha the prophet, yet not one of them was cleansed—only Naaman the Syrian."

All the people in the synagogue were furious when they heard this. They got up, drove him out of the town, and took him to the brow of the hill on which the town was built, in order to throw him off the cliff. But he walked right through the crowd and went on his way.

Luke 4:24–30

Why did Jesus bring this up? He mentions two Gentile places: Sidon and Syria. Two Gentile locations where Elijah and Elisha moved. Where they were received. And two women were instrumental in widening the table outside the nation of Israel. A widow in Elijah's time and an enslaved girl in Elisha's time are two daughters who are sewn into the fabric of the story. A widow and a young girl. The least of these, remembered by Jesus. Jesus was ushering in God's kingdom in a way Jewish ears didn't want to hear. And maybe we can't blame them. Jesus was speaking to the Jewish people, who were under the oppression of Roman rule. Of Gentile reign. They had a long and painful history of being oppressed by outside nations, and there Jesus was, telling them God was letting these other nations—these Gentile nations—into the kingdom of heaven. This was outrageous. The Messiah was supposed to only bless the Jews! Not outsiders.

But as James Bryan Smith points out, Jesus came to flip the script on who the kingdom of heaven belongs to:

Those who would enter the kingdom of God comprised an exclusive club: they were Jewish, male, religiously upright, healthy and wealthy. Jesus' ministry ran counter to this narrative. Jesus blessed the poor, touched lepers, healed and forgave Gentiles (even female Gentiles), and notoriously sinful females![4]

Daughter, do not underestimate the power of your faith, your compassion, your voice in the face of oppression, fear, and exile. One sentence out of the mouth of a daughter can change an entire life. What you see in front of you matters. How you respond in a dark, terrible situation matters. The way you handle yourself and choose compassion and justice and righteousness and humility in the face of oppression matters. God loves to speak with his daughters, to anoint his daughters for hard tasks, to bring sweeping changes in the city because of his daughters. May we consider the enslaved girl often and emulate her brave faith.

11

The Marginalized

We Are Valuable

And Mary said:
> "My soul glorifies the Lord
> and my spirit rejoices in God my Savior,
> for he has been mindful
> of the humble state of his servant."

Luke 1:46–48

He chose a woman.

God, the most creative Being in all of existence, the Alpha and Omega, the Beginning and End, could have chosen any kind of way to enter into His beloved creation.

He chose a feminine body.

God humbled Himself, folded His glory into the creases of thick baby thighs, allowed Himself the full experience and dependence of growing in utero, of needing everything to sustain Him, from the umbilical cord connected to Mary's body to the milk from her breasts, and required His body to be taken care of, cradled, wiped, and held.

He chose the least of these.

Women were seen as just above slaves in the pecking order of society, but God put her first. First to hold His infant body against her teenage own. She was young, unmarried, living in the hill country. He trusted a young woman to care for His needs, to carry Him around, to attend to His every cry. He trusted His daughter not to drop Him, to keep Him safe, to hold Him close. He adores His daughters and entrusted Himself to one of us to house Him and raise Him and to teach Him how to walk. The wonders of God and His will and His ways never cease to amaze me. Eve cradled the fruit that brought separation, but Mary cradled the baby who brought restoration.

"God's powerful Spirit, that Spirit who brooded over the waters on Earth's Opening Day, would brood over her and create a miracle in her womb," writes Scot McKnight in *The Real Mary*.[1] What a powerful image to remember. The same Spirit who created the world created the redemption of that same world inside a teenage girl.

After a rather frightening angel appeared to her, she ran. She ran to find another woman who would listen, rejoice, take it all in detail by detail. The way you'd call your girl-friend and start with, "You're never going to believe what just happened!" And you can't even believe it yourself.

After the squealing, then came the singing.

Mary's song has long been studied and admired by many. And yes, even banned by governments.[2] Why?

Because she sings a song of justice.

He has brought down rulers from their thrones
    but has lifted up the humble.
He has filled the hungry with good things
    but has sent the rich away empty.
He has helped his servant Israel,
    remembering to be merciful
to Abraham and his descendants forever,
    just as he promised our ancestors.

Luke 1:52–55

She was singing about the upside-down kingdom, where the poor are blessed and the rich rulers walk away empty-handed. Where the powerful kings like Herod the Great were going to be sent away with nothing. This was indeed good news to her and to those oppressed in Israel under Roman rule. And she was brought in on it all, with an angel whispering a secret in her ears about Who she was carrying in her body and what she was going to do.

Her song spoke of hope, of justice, of redemption, of awakening, of revival, of glorifying the Lord, who is mindful of the humble.

Did she picture her son, sword in hand, powerfully bringing the Roman rule to ruins? Would she have imagined proudly looking on as her son sat on a royal throne, scepter in hand? Would some kind of powerful picture of kingship have been in her mind?

She may have never guessed that the bringing of justice meant death for her boy. Mary had to learn, like us all, what Jesus meant about being the Messiah. That He came to suffer, to be killed, to die. And then to be resurrected. This was the sword that would pierce her soul (see Luke 2:35).

———

She knew who He was. Every mother knows her child like the back of her hand. And she had begun the impossible task of seeing her young son now as a grown man. Of adjusting her vision to the reality that Jesus was grown. And was stepping into His ministry. As the Messiah. Of grappling with what kind of Messiah He would be.

Those of us who are mothers can imagine one of the hardest things to embrace would have been the fact that Jesus was on His Father's watch, not hers.

He had always been on her watch. Jesus was her boy, her sweet little rough-and-tumble boy. Her firstborn. The one who made her a mother. Firstborns break mothers in, in a way no other child can do. They teach us as much about being a mother as we teach them about being a human. She had poured her heart and soul into feeding Him, keeping Him safe, and teaching Him how to help around the house, wash His hands, and put on His shoes. She sang Him all the Hebrew nursery rhymes, all the Jewish melodies sung over her and her mother and her mother's mother.

So how did the mother of Jesus also learn, just like us, the unfolding reality that Jesus is the Messiah? How did she grasp—like we daughters do—the truth that she once saw Jesus one way but then learned a new way to see Him? The way we might have known Jesus as meek and mild but then saw Him flipping tables and schooling scholars on the law?

I remember the first time my oldest put on a suit jacket. He was instantly transformed. He looked like his father. Tall, handsome, strong. It caught my breath. He had also wanted a bow tie for the occasion, and I was clueless. And his dad was at work. So my best girlfriend, who knows so many different kinds of magic, including how to tie a bow tie, came right over and—looking up to my boy—tied his tie. She's like an aunt to him. And we were both teary. What had just happened? Both of our boys, just a minute ago, were building Lego sets, drawing maps for imaginary treasures, setting traps for nerf wars. And here they were, grown with ties on. Was this how Mary felt at the wedding at Cana? One minute her son was shooting marbles in the backyard with the neighborhood boys, the next ready to save the day?

We want them to grow up and we don't. I wonder about that tension in Mary's heart. Wanting to cover Him with her wings but wanting Him to fly. Wanting Him to explore and get dirty and wanting to catch Him from falling. Wanting Him to experience the world and wanting to shield Him from it.

She knew who her boy was, and she knew who He could be. She saw His strength, brilliance, potential. And today, she was going to call Him higher.

"They have no more wine," (John 2:3) she said to him. We don't know much more—why they ran out, why the newlywed couple was in this position of running out, why Mary knew. Was she a relative of the wedding party? Was she being that nosy aunt in the kitchen? Did the wedding couple know they ran out, or just Mary?

Either way, there was a problem. And she took it to her son.

"Woman, why do you involve me? . . . My hour has not yet come" (John 2:4). I know—at first glance, this can feel disrespectful. But the footnote in the NIV clarifies that "the Greek for *Woman* does not denote any disrespect."[3] However, it is a clear moment of Jesus telling His mom He has a different timeline than she has for Him. Which is a hard pill to swallow for mommas.

Mary's heart might arguably be the most complex treasure chest of all of humankind. Singing the songs of redemption, of liberation from oppression, of her very own blessing as the mother of the Messiah. But also constantly moved, displaced, beloved, and bewildered as she mentors the Messiah and then, somehow, is mentored by the Messiah.

"Do whatever he tells you," (John 2:5) Mary told the servants. The words tumbled out easily, too easily. As if they were pressed against the door, waiting, listening—falling headfirst into the room. These words were birthed inside her years before. When the angel came, the bright light, the revelation of growing God inside her very imperfect, young, feminine body. And she said she was the Lord's servant. And here she was.

She knew "words create worlds,"[4] as Abraham Joshua Heschel has put it, the way God spoke and it was so in the garden. And if her son wanted to create something out of nothing, He could. If He wanted to take the shame of an embarrassed newlywed couple who ran out of wine and turn it into glory and grace, He could. If He wanted to turn this dance party up to eleven, He could. If He wanted to inaugurate the coming of a new covenant with new wine, He could. If He wanted to start off a chat about water and wine here and continue the living water discussion with a woman at a well a few pages later, He could. If He said the word, then it was.

She boldly mothered her son, asking Him to do a miracle because she knew who He is and what He came for. She still had an angel's words scrawled on her heart, telling her who her son is. And yet. The complexity is thick.

She parented God and, in turn, was parented by God. The mutual ministry of being the mother of Jesus and Jesus being her Messiah. How much more complex can it possibly become? Her body housed God; God housed her soul. Mary was tasked with holding every kind of feeling possible all inside her heart, her treasure chest.

And we honor her.

We honor the push and pull, of knowing when to say something or to stay silent. We honor the nuance of the now and not yet. We honor her eye for detail, her compassion for a newly married couple who was about to feel shame upon their entire marriage for letting the wine run dry at their feast, for walking straight up to her boy and saying, "Fix it, Jesus." We honor her courage to ask.

And we honor her persistence. Because Jesus told her it wasn't time for Him to do things like this yet. But Mary? She made a faith-filled move in the face of possible defeat. By faith, she told the servants to do whatever Jesus told them.

It was a gamble. What she said to the servants was risky. Because Jesus could have told them nothing at all. Jesus could have walked away. Jesus could have said "it's not my time" and stuck to it.

But He didn't.

And the first miracle was keeping a party going. Was ushering in a new era with new wine. Was Jesus proving His power and authority over the natural?

It all took place because Mary came to Jesus with a problem. Maybe it felt small, but it's clearly monumental.

Friend, when you come boldly, like Mary, to Jesus with a problem, you walk in the footsteps of the mother of God. When your heart is full of wonder, anxiety, fear, problem solving, hope, and despair? Mary just gave you permission to take it all and to flop it at the feet of Jesus. Without shame. Without condemnation. Without fear. It's clear Jesus is patient and kind and that He compassionately listens. Which is what Love looks like. And the Father's love for His daughters never fails (see 1 Corinthians 13:8).

We see Mary one other time in the narrative before the last time we see her at the cross. Oh what a mother's heart can hold. Her son, being wrongfully accused. Being beaten. Being pummeled. Being abused. How was she able to stand it?

One of the most beautiful parts of it all on that brutal day? Jesus's love for His momma.

Mary not only was watching her son die, she was watching her dreams die, too. I imagine she felt the layers of loss— the loss of never seeing her son succeed in a way she had dreamed, of accomplishing great things she had envisioned for Him, of even her own safety and her hope to grow old in His house as was custom in the multigenerational culture they lived in. Of her dream of being taken care of by her son in her old age.

Jesus saw it all. And he provided for her on earth, as He is in heaven. As He was dying for her spiritual freedom, He also provided for her earthly needs. He provided for her in the cosmic courtroom, removing her guilt and shame, and He provided for her in the earthly need of housing and family.

He was on the cross, suffocating. Hardly a breath to spare. Suffering and struggling. And He used some of His last, faint breaths to speak. To make an arrangement. He forced out words in order to take care of His mother. Because He loved her so much, he died for her, too.

> Near the cross of Jesus stood his mother, his mother's sister, Mary the wife of Clopas, and Mary Magdalene. When Jesus saw his mother there, and the disciple whom he loved standing nearby, he said to her, "Woman, here is your son," and to the disciple, "Here is your mother." From that time on, this disciple took her into his home.
>
> John 19:25–27

Again, we see *Woman* here, and no disrespect is detected. In fact, we only see affection. He took care of His mother in His final hours with His final breaths. Oh the depths of the riches of His love!

He asked the disciple whom He loved—John—to take in His mother. He passed on His position of caretaking, making sure she was fully taken care of. What a love they had for one another.

We daughters stand upon her shoulders. The beloved mother of Jesus. The one who had to walk the path of raising and letting go, of learning and unlearning who her son was, of parenting the King of Kings and being parented by that same King. The one who made a million mistakes, sinned, wondered, cried, hoped, prayed, watched, fumbled, and followed. Like you and me.

I take great comfort in knowing Mary had to sort through a host of emotions all the time, like me. That she probably pictured one thing for her children and got the opposite. There have been so many times I have imagined one thing for my child, and something else was the result. Or one thing for my career, and I was handed something much different. I dreamed about something in my life, and it turned out another way. Mary was no stranger to this path. But just like Mary, sometimes what we dreamed up for our child was not about our child. It was about us.

Or sometimes our dreams are nothing close to God's dreams. And again, like Mary, we are being formed into the likeness of God's heart. His heart is opposed to the world's desire for prestige, power, privilege. The Father has often taken my misaligned dreams for a child (dreams that had more prestige attached to them than I care to admit) and gently showed me His way is higher, His path forms character, and this suffering my child is walking through is not wasted. After all, didn't the Father take His son's suffering and turn it into salvation?

After Jesus's death and resurrection, the book of Acts tells us Mary followed Him as God, like the rest of us (see Acts 1:13–16, Acts 2:1). That she was counted a follower, a disciple, an apprentice of His, who received the gift of the Spirit and was a part of the first church. All while living in an ordained and blessed housing arrangement from her son, and her King.

What a beloved mother, sister, and daughter she was. We honor Mary, the mother of God. We adore her humanity and take comfort in her learning. We learn with the very mother of God.

12

The Sisterhood

We Were Created for Community

At that time Mary got ready and hurried to a town in the
hill country of Judea, where she entered Zechariah's home
and greeted Elizabeth. When Elizabeth heard Mary's greeting, the baby leaped in her womb, and Elizabeth was filled
with the Holy Spirit.

Luke 1:39–41

I tried seminary once before.

And dropped out.

I had three young kids at the time and was on staff with
a church. And with each passing day, it all felt heavier and
harder, but I kept going. I kept pressing. I kept trying. I wasn't
a quitter. Until I was.

I think the hardest part was admitting my need for support
and community to keep going. I felt alone.

God did not design His daughters to be alone. In anything. Remember the first thing that God said wasn't good? Being alone. He is called our Father, we are His daughters, and we belong to a family.

And one of the biggest gifts of a family is sisterhood.

So when my friend Vivian reached out and asked, "Have you ever wanted to go to seminary but couldn't figure out how to make it work?" I cried.

Yes, Viv, I have. And it didn't work.

Vivian's heart and dream was to create a cohort of women who would link arms and learn together in a seminary setting. Because the pressures and expectations of being a woman are heavy enough. Heap on top a male-saturated seminary environment, and it can feel lonely being one of a few. She saw a supportive sisterhood as being one of the keys to success.

I am here to tell you it absolutely is.

As soon as our eighteen-woman text thread started for Denver Seminary, I wondered how this might all go down. We are in the first Denver Seminary Women's Leadership Cohort—we are all in leadership in some way as Bible teachers, authors, pastors, and speakers, and we are the guinea pigs for this program.

This had so much potential to go down in flames.

We know women can be the greatest source of collaboration and strength and the greatest source of competition, backbiting, and gossip. Which would we be?

I'm here to report we are a community that decided early on to celebrate one another, cheer on our ministries, and link arms and fight against our common enemy, not become one another's enemy. We weep with those who weep (about deadlines or raising humans or hard marriages or ministry complexity) and rejoice with those who rejoice when we see the clear goodness and grace of God all over our lives.

As we stressed about our very first eight-page research paper, I knew if nothing else, we were going to get an A+ in community. Even if we bombed our papers (no one did).

When daughters decide to link arms and fight together, they are unstoppable. When daughters vulnerably come with their weakness and are met with compassion, they are unbeatable. When daughters seek the wellness of one another, checking in on the tears they see in class—knowing a heartstring was struck with one of their sisters—they are unassailable.

Which is why I think God gave Mary to Elizabeth, and Elizabeth to Mary. They needed a sisterhood in the face of the greatest news ever reported. Because the greatest opposition was also at hand. These two women were tasked to carry and raise sons who would change the course of history. In the middle of being under the oppressive thumb of Roman rule. One boy would call for repentance and pave the way for the other—One who would carry out redemption for the whole world. These women carried the weight of glory inside their bodies. And God gave them a friend, a sister, in this tall task. What a compassionate, self-giving God we have!

Ezers need each other, swords in hand, ready to defend one another, to sing over one another, to bless and celebrate and fight for one another.

If I had to choose which angel I would be, it would be Gabriel, hands down. He had the best job. In the book of Luke we see him arrive to tell Zechariah that his prayer of longing to father a child had been answered. And when he questioned how this could be, Gabriel responded, "Listen. I stand in the presence of the Lord. I have been sent to speak to you and tell you this good news. This is why you can trust me. But also, since you didn't believe me, you're going to have to remain silent until this all comes to pass."

And Elizabeth got pregnant in her old age.

Can you just picture Gabriel with a wry smile, nodding an I-told-you-so, when Zechariah realized it had all come to pass?

Next stop on Gabriel's itinerary: a teenage girl. But not just any girl. Elizabeth's relative. This was about to be a family affair. And I imagine Gabriel was going to have some fun with his greeting, complete with a few layers of good news.

Six months into Elizabeth's pregnancy, Mary was greeted by Gabriel.

> "Greetings, you who are highly favored! The Lord is with you." Mary was greatly troubled at his words and wondered what kind of greeting this might be. But the angel said to her, "Do not be afraid, Mary; you have found favor with God. You will conceive and give birth to a son, and you are to call him Jesus. He will be great and will be called the Son of the Most High. The Lord God will give him the throne of his father David, and he will reign over Jacob's descendants forever; his kingdom will never end."
>
> Luke 1:28–33

It's quite a moment. Naturally Mary, trying to wrap her teenage mind around this encounter, has some questions. So she asks Gabriel how in the world this is going to all pan out, since she's a virgin and all. The math doesn't add up.

We might wonder if in this moment Mary would also receive Zechariah's silencing. Because he asked a question, too. But hers was not a question lacking faith. It seems to be out of genuine wonderment. And Gabriel answered her one question with two answers, full of generosity and kindness. And full of sisterhood.

Answer one: *So get ready for this*—"*the Holy Spirit will come on you, and the power of the Most High will overshadow you*" (Luke 1:35). *And wham*—*that's how it's done on earth as it is in heaven.*

Answer two: *Also, guess what, Mary?! Elizabeth, your relative, is actually six months pregnant right now. I know—crazy! You both are pregnant with really significant baby boys. Nothing is impossible with God (like you two having babies). Have fun!* (paraphrase mine)

Gabriel told her about the Spirit and a friend. This is good news upon good news. He gave her so much good news in that moment, I wonder if this is what Christmas is supposed to feel like. Shock, awe, delight, surprises. She's pregnant and will carry God's son. The Holy Spirit is upon her. And her cousin is pregnant for the first time, right along with her, in it for the full experience, pregnancy and all!

Mary didn't waste any time and hurried to the hill country to find Elizabeth. Her feet couldn't carry her fast enough, the way our fingers can't dial our best friend fast enough when we just got that job, that test score, those positive blood test results, that good news.

Cue the squealing and hugging and crying. Sisterhood at its finest.

At the sound of Mary's greeting, Elizabeth's child leaped within her, and Elizabeth was filled with the Holy Spirit. Elizabeth gave a glad cry and exclaimed to Mary, "God has blessed you above all women, and your child is blessed. Why am I so honored, that the mother of my Lord should visit me? When I heard your greeting, the baby in my womb jumped for joy. You are blessed because you believed that the Lord would do what he said."

Luke 1:41–45 NLT

To my knowledge, no woman was recorded as being filled with the Spirit in the Old Testament. So Elizabeth, with her full womb, is the first woman the Spirit of God fills—and the result is a "glad cry." Code for loud, high-pitched girly squeal.

Can you imagine how much fun the Father had watching His daughters figure all of this out? He had wrapped up this gift of sisterhood for Mary and Elizabeth long before the beginning of time. These two women, decades apart, first-time moms with unlikely pregnancies as a virgin teen and a barren woman, in this together. He loves to give good gifts (Matthew 7:11 says so), and you know He was smiling ear to ear. He didn't want them to be alone in the greatest rescue plan the Father, Son, and Spirit had cooked up. And the gift of sisterhood is for our encouragement. Which literally means we infuse courage into one another. We put courage in others through community.

The more this story unfolds, the more we can put a few tools in our pocket for today. As we watch Mary and Elizabeth in this moment, what makes the gift of sisterhood work? *Proximity* and *blessing*. These two ingredients make sisterhood thrive.

Proximity

Mary wasted no time getting to Elizabeth. But she could have stayed put. So often we let insecurity rule us, keeping us stuck. Mary could have gotten in her own head about it all. *Would Elizabeth want me to come? She's probably busy.*

And plus, she's older and pregnant and probably really tired. I don't want to be a burden. I don't want to show up unannounced. I don't want to be that girl.

Insecurity makes it about us. But Mary knew this wasn't about her. This was about God and who He is and what He was doing. And so she headed to the hills to sit with Elizabeth to rejoice in their God.

My seminary sisters are all over the country. We are in different time zones, have different cultural backgrounds, have different skin colors and ethnicities and stories. We have plenty of reasons to stay far away from each other, to put up fences, to stay inside in our own comfortable living rooms.

Proximity, by definition, isn't just being physically close, though it can be. According to the *Merriam-Webster Unabridged Dictionary*, it's nearness in "time, place, relationship."[1] Choosing to move in close to our sisters, to open our hearts, to share needs and joys and revelations and annoyances—this makes us close. Though I would much prefer to run to any one of their houses and stay three months the way Mary did, our lives can't afford that. But technology has allowed a proximity that we all took advantage of, and sisterhood was born. We moved in close.

Blessing

Sometimes if we hear good news about a sister, our first reaction isn't to bless them, it's comparison. It's to wonder why we didn't get that same declaration upon us. That same promotion. That same relationship. That same good fortune. That same house. That same car. And we slip into cursing instead of blessing.

But Elizabeth leads the way in the gift of sisterhood. She blesses. She blesses a young, unmarried pregnant girl who had the gift of a baby inside her body way younger than Elizabeth did. She could have focused on why Mary got to be pregnant in her young years and how she was now pregnant with creaky knees and back pain and arthritis. But she blesses. She could have focused on all she did not have and all that Mary had. But she blesses. She could have been salty that she was only carrying the one who paved the way for the Messiah and not the Messiah Himself. But she blesses.

And because she blesses? Mary sings. When we bless our sisters, our sisters can sing the song of their lifetime. Don't withhold the blessing. Don't withhold moving in, getting close, choosing proximity. And don't miss the gift of blessing your sister. She sings because of your blessing.

We are singing, my seminary sisters and I. We are trying, failing, crying, laughing, singing. We are not singing perfectly. We have some things we are certainly stumbling over. We are messy, broken, doubting, confused, weak, and wanting. But we are still singing, because our sisters have bought in and blessed one another. May we take our cues from the great duo in the Advent story and give the gift of sisterhood. The enemy has nothing on us ezers if we bless one another.

13

The Condemned

We Are Covered by His Love

Let him return to the LORD, that he may have
compassion on him,
and to our God, for he will abundantly pardon.

Isaiah 55:7 ESV

When was the last time you were caught doing something you were not supposed to be doing?

I remember having a wide stance, arm cocked back, eyes on the prize. I was about to whip another toilet paper roll over the top of the oak tree in my ex's front yard, like the third baseman I was. And just as I was about to launch another killer throw, I was hit. By the beam of light from a car. A police car. I thought my life was over. Was I about to spend the night in the slammer for the taste of revenge on an ex-boyfriend? Why did I just freeze and my friends took flight? Was this the beginning of a life of crime? (It wasn't, in case you're wondering. And after a frozen moment, I too ran. The police didn't even bother getting out of their car for some stupid high school girls pranking a boy.)

Being caught doing something you shouldn't do, whether silly toilet papering or seriously breaking trust, can bring on the shame. Guilt. Condemnation.

And this one is for our shame.

For our guilt.

For the things we don't want to say out loud.

For the judgment from others that feels like it just might kill us.

She was going to die here, right here, right now.

Her heart felt like a herd of elephants stampeding their way through a dry desert. But her body stood frozen. Her brain went off-line. She was the most disintegrated she had ever felt in her life. She could feel the judgment in the air. Her neighbors were sizing her up. Anger, condemnation, self-righteousness was surging through the crowd. Out of the corner of her teary eyes, she saw some of them pick up rocks. What started out as a night with someone who she thought loved her was ending as her worst nightmare.

> At dawn he appeared again in the temple courts, where all the people gathered around him, and he sat down to teach them. The teachers of the law and the Pharisees brought in a woman caught in adultery. They made her stand before the group and said to Jesus, "Teacher, this woman was caught in the act of adultery. In the Law Moses commanded us to stone such women. Now what do you say?" They were using this question as a trap, in order to have a basis for accusing him.
>
> John 8:2–6

She was a pawn in a religious chess match. Bait for a trap.

No one was thinking about her story. About the abuse she had endured, the lack of support, the need for healing, the trauma. The very real human desire of wanting to be loved. That's what she wanted. But she had been used. She had one million insecurities, and here she was, destroying marriages. She didn't set out to do this, to be this, to live this way. No one was thinking about her story.

Except Jesus.

He was writing a new chapter for her in the dirt.

> But Jesus bent down and started to write on the ground with his finger. When they kept on questioning him, he straightened up and said to them, "Let any one of you who is without sin be the first to throw a stone at her." Again he stooped down and wrote on the ground.
>
> John 8:6–8

The theories about what Jesus was writing in the sand that morning are all over the map. So I'll add mine. Could He have been writing a new story for His daughter? A story that said she didn't have to keep living this way, stuck in a life that led to destruction? Could He have been gently, graciously, compassionately writing a story of life over death, of freedom over traps?

If you are hiding something in your life, if you are stuck in a pattern you want to be free from, if you wonder if the shame and the guilt will keep you from ever changing—Jesus has never, ever, not even one time ever, said you can't change. He's the King of Comebacks. And He always gives you the grace to do so.

The moment Jesus bent down, the whole narrative shifted. With one small move, every eye that was staring at the woman shifted to Jesus. Jesus bent down and absorbed her shame. He absorbed her condemnation. He absorbed her judgment. This moment of humility foreshadowed the cross, where once and for all Jesus would take on our shame and trade it for grace.

Jesus loves choosing compassion over condemnation.

But the mob was seething, ready to snap shut their trap onto this so-called Savior. And not only upon Him, but on her. They thought it would make for a good lesson—a good story to use to scrub the stains of society clean again. *See what happens? Don't be like her.*

But Jesus can't be trapped. He can't be cornered. He can't be contained. Even death couldn't hold Him down. His light pierces darkness, His life crushes deceit, His mercy triumphs over judgment, His love trumps condemnation. He said, "The sinless one among you, go first: Throw the stone" (John 8:6–8 MSG).

N. T. Wright says this is often called The Woman Caught in Adultery, but it ought to be called The Men Caught in Hypocrisy.[1] Jesus took the trap set for Him and flipped it on its head. As the woman stood there, she quickly did the math. And it added up to . . . zero. No one. No one could throw a stone. No one could claim to be sinless, right? Or would the religious guys be able to because they were so pure? Could someone throw a stone?

The wind had changed, and a ripple of silence went through the crowd, like unruly waves being hushed by their Maker. They couldn't win this one. And one by one, starting with those who had seen the most life, they left the area. Thuds and thumps of large rocks came from angry hands dropping heavy stones. No one could hold a stone, let alone hurl one.

She felt the exhale leave her body, the way darkness scrambles out of the room when a lamp is lit. As she released fear for the first time in years, her legs began to wobble; she was about to faint. Was this real?

She was saved.

Jesus had mastered the mob.

Just as quickly as it had formed, the crowd thinned.

And now, no one was left.

Here she was. Alone. With Jesus. And there was no telling what He might do next. Unpredictable, clearly persuasive, full of mystery. Who was He?

He turned to face her, compassion in His eyes, and asked simply:

"Woman, where are they? Does no one condemn you?"

"No one, Master."

"Neither do I," said Jesus. "Go on your way. From now on, don't sin."

John 8:9–11 MSG

"Does no one condemn you? Neither do I."

Imagine Jesus whispering those words to you every single morning when you open your eyes. These words can be your lifeline, just as they likely were for the woman who encountered Jesus that day. Let Jesus speak these words over you with kindness from a King who loves mercy over judgment.

"Go and leave your life of sin."

I wonder if this was the first time she ever had someone say to her, "You don't have to live this way." I wonder if no one had ever looked her in the eyes and told her she could leave this life that was destroying her and destroying others.

I wonder if no one had ever considered her whole story and seen the trauma and the heartache and the trail of damage done to her and to others and said, "Leave it all and start over."

Because that's what Jesus did. When He told her to leave her life of sin, He was calling it what it was. Sin separates us from God and from others and leads to death. She was leading a life that was on a path to death. And He was offering life. Grace always leaves a trail of life in its wake. Grace picks you up and says you can change. Grace calls it what it is and gives you the strength to make it different. My pastor often says God is not interested in making bad people good, He is interested in making dead people live. That's what grace does. Grace gives endless second chances. Grace says you don't have to live this way. Grace says there is a path that leads to life, and you can have it.

The woman in the story is living proof of Jesus's mercy. She was given a new chance, a fresh start, a new path out of the darkness of shame, of deceit, of those who would capture her and trap her and use her for their gain.

The same is true for you.

There are days I wake up to accusing thoughts—from myself or from others—and I have a choice. I can either make the voices of others my soundtrack, or I can hit pause while I choose a new playlist. God has a soundtrack for His daughters, and it starts with compassion. Compassion over condemnation, affirmation over accusation. He died for us because He loves us. He didn't come to condemn us; He came to save us.

I also think about a soundtrack that she heard that day, one that likely was forever seared in her mind. Author Bryan Crum points out how the sound of the stones thudding to the ground that day stayed with her.[2] If the crowd had been ready, stones in hand, then they had to drop them as they left. And in that moment, could the Spirit of God have been reframing this traumatic incident in her life, loosening the shame in her soul with each stone hitting the sand? Could the thuds of the stones become a song for her soul? A soundtrack as she walked out her comeback? God loves to give us songs of life and truth and grace. Zephaniah 3:17 (NLV) says so: "The Lord your God is with you, a Powerful One Who wins the battle. He will have much joy over you. With His love He will give you new life. He will have joy over you with loud singing."

I imagine that with each thud the Spirit of God was affirming her daughtership. Her Father was giving her a soundtrack of truth for her soul:

Thud.
"You are free."
Thud.
"You are not too far gone."
Thud.
"You are my Daughter."
Thud.
"You are not stuck."
Thud.
"You are forgiven."
Thud.
"You are delightful."
Thud.
"My grace is enough."
Thud.
"Go and live."

Thud.

"Be made new."

Thud.

"You are my beloved."

Thud.

"I will redeem this."

But could she believe it? Can you believe it? This is part of your healing. Healing is the practice of believing a different story about yourself. Healing is choosing a different soundtrack to walk to each morning. Healing is choosing to believe the truth. Healing is choosing to walk by faith and not by narratives spoken over us that keep us trapped in shame.

When a house is deemed condemned by the government, it is no longer seen fit to be inhabited by anyone. It is declared no longer acceptable for housing and does not meet the standard for living. There are usually papers on the door and signs telling the neighborhood to steer clear of the property. It is condemned. And in church, *condemnation* is a big scary word. It means to have a strong disapproval, to be punished, and to be declared no longer acceptable. But Paul, in his greatest discourse, says it this way: "Therefore, there is now no condemnation for those who are in Christ Jesus" (Romans 8:1). N. T. Wright puts it this way:

> And the word we use for our utter reliance on the cross, our total dependance on what was done there for us, is the same word Paul uses for the faithfulness which the Messiah enacted there in the first place. "Faith." The faith which looks at the cross and believes that there the living and loving God gave his only son for us—that faith is the one and only badge of the whole people of God, the sign under which Jew and Greek come together, slave and free become

one, male and female stand side by side on even ground in Abraham's forgiven family, the Spirit-led children of God. Faith is the Messiah-badge, and for its wearers there is no condemnation.[3]

"Faith is the Messiah-badge." Believing we are no longer condemned is the badge we wear that keeps our chin up. This badge is our faith in the work Jesus did to remove our condemnation and declare us acceptable and free as sons and daughters and heirs.

Jesus's work on the cross removed any punishment we deserve for not living up to the standard God has set and the law code laid out. Our punishment for breaking the laws—our condemnation—has been paid for and removed. Jesus is the fulfillment of the whole law. He is the perfect human, fully living out what the law spelled out. And because of His life and His sacrifice? He said we can now have His righteousness. It's the great exchange. Because of Jesus, we are now declared acceptable by God!

We are now met with the compassion of God instead of the condemnation for our sin. This is the Father heart of God. So when we blow it and make a mess of things? When we say we are free but wander back into oppression? When the woman may have dipped her toes back into the dark even though Jesus told her to go and sin no more? When we want to live as changed, forgiven, redeemed, Spirit-led people but end up obeying our flesh instead? What now? Condemnation?

Nope. This is when we look down on our spiritual lapel and check our Messiah-badge. Yep, still there. Not condemned. Free. Forgiven. Loved. Accepted. Daughter. And we can turn back around and come home to our Father, again.

Eugene Peterson, in his Message paraphrase of the Bible, put it this way when it comes to standing no longer condemned, to living freely by God's grace, and to claiming our daughtership:

> This resurrection life you received from God is not a timid, grave-tending life. It's adventurously expectant, greeting God with a childlike "What's next, Papa?" God's Spirit touches our spirits and confirms who we really are. We know who he is, and we know who we are: Father and children. And we know we are going to get what's coming to us—an unbelievable inheritance! We go through exactly what Christ goes through. If we go through the hard times with him, then we're certainly going to go through the good times with him!
>
> Romans 8:15–17 MSG

When we know who we are and who our Father is, we aren't asking "Will you love me again?" or "Can you find space for me?" or "How can I ever please you again?" Daughters who are free and trust the Father's love for them don't need to ask these questions. Daughters who are no longer condemned get to ask a different question altogether.

Our question gets to be this: "What's next, Papa?"

14

The Disciple Sisters

We Are Disciples

Jesus said to her [Martha], "I am the resurrection and the life. The one who believes in me will live, even though they die; and whoever lives by believing in me will never die. Do you believe this?"

John 11:25–26

In the church world, Martha has gotten a bad rap. She's a worrier. Full of anxiety. The opposite of faith-filled. So when people hint that you are more of a Martha than a Mary, you read between the lines. They are saying you aren't exactly who God has in mind when it comes to being spiritual. Everybody knows that.

But then I came across a brilliant moment with Martha and Jesus that I hadn't ever taken note of before. It's just the two of them. And it shifted everything. It brought healing and hope. I hope it heals something inside of you, too.

His fever wasn't giving up.

But neither were his sisters.

Lazarus was in and out, with a rising temperature. His beloved sisters, Martha and Mary, were doing everything they knew to do: herbs and cold cloths and keeping him comfortable. They prayed. They cleaned. They made broth. They opened windows. They shut windows. They paced. They prayed more.

But things weren't looking good. And they knew it. They looked at each other and knew they needed Jesus. He was the healer. They had both learned so much from Him. They knew who He was and what He could do. They loved Jesus, and Jesus loved them (John 11:5). So they sent for Him.

When Jesus heard that Lazarus was sick, the disciples expected Him to pack up and head out immediately. He loved Lazarus. But when did Jesus ever do what was expected of Him?

Jesus didn't come right away. In fact, He stayed where He was. For *two* more whole days. He could have come. He didn't hesitate when others had asked Him to come heal their sick daughter or sick mother-in-law.

But He waited forty-eight precious hours.

The most confusing and torturous message Jesus sent back to Mary and Martha: silence.

Jesus didn't come when they asked Him to come. He ghosted Mary and Martha. What in the world? He loved this family—all three siblings—so very much. So why the silence? Why the delay? Lazarus was dying! Why the waiting? What was more important than a life-or-death situation?

After those two days, as much as they had prayed and hoped and done all they could, Lazarus didn't make it. Jesus didn't come. And Mary didn't move. Her own brother was gone, and her friend Jesus didn't show up. Grief, shock, confusion, and ache left her foggy and despondent. Paralyzed with grief.

But Martha? She was always on the move. She got up and went to find Jesus. She had questions. She had big feelings. She had a few things to say.

She traveled to where He was.

Finally seeing Jesus from a distance, she quickened her step. And coming face-to-face with Him she declared, "Lord, if you had been here, my brother would not have died. But even now I know that whatever you ask from God, God will give you" (John 11:21–22 ESV).

Her honesty showed up, the way it did the day she asked Jesus to have Mary help her in the kitchen with all the hosting and cooking. But her belief and trust and faith showed up, too. She knew—she believed—God would give Jesus anything He asked. What profound faith Martha had, even after her brother had breathed his last breath.

And in this moment of bravery and belief? Jesus revealed to her a foundational truth that would be quoted for centuries to come.

This claim Jesus made wasn't in a sermon in front of a crowd. It wasn't with the twelve disciples. This was a quiet moment, a personal conversation Jesus had with Martha about who He is. He told her, not any other disciple. Not a group of men. He spoke profound spiritual truths to Martha, who is often pigeonholed as too worldly focused. Martha, who has been said to have been only concerned about domestic affairs and not spiritual truths. Martha, too busy for spirituality. Martha, who has often been flattened to a one-dimensional character, now comes to life in this encounter.

Face-to-face, Jesus offered Martha a comforting truth in a despairing time: "I am the resurrection and the life. The one who believes in me will live, even though they die. . . . Do you believe this?" (John 11:25–26). Jesus shared a huge theological claim with Martha. And then He tenderly drew her out with a question. *Do you believe this?* This wasn't a monologue on a hill, this was a dialogue with a friend. He cared for her, and He wanted to hear from her in this discussion.

What dignity and honor He gave His daughters. He didn't talk down to her. He didn't patronize her. He didn't mansplain to her. It was an emotional moment, where Martha had a chance to say whatever she wanted back to Jesus. Martha's friendship with Jesus invites you to talk honestly with Him, too. And to believe He will never patronize you, talk down to you, belittle you. He is here for every single one of your emotions and will feel them with you. He won't write you off as too emotional to think, either. He honors your mind, your intellect, your curiosity. Like He did with Martha.

Just like Peter, who made the bold claim that Jesus is the Messiah, Martha had her own moment of declaration: "Yes, Lord . . . I believe that you are the Messiah, the Son of God, who is to come into the world" (John 11:27). Peter makes the same claim in Matthew. And after Peter's confession, there is a turning point in Matthew's Gospel where Jesus begins His journey to the cross. Similarly, in this moment here with Martha, we see the same pattern. Martha declares Jesus is the Messiah, and after this, the religious leaders plot to kill Jesus. This is followed by Mary anointing Jesus's feet with pure nard, as a sign of his coming burial (see John 12:1–3; both Lazarus and Martha are present at this anointing).

Both Martha and Peter have pivotal and defining moments in the Gospel stories. Both confess Jesus is the Christ. Both are part of the turning toward Jesus's death. Both have moments of courageous faith.

This is a moment of faith, hope, and love in Martha's life. Jesus doesn't shun her frustration and grief or her desires and hopes for her brother, who has just passed. Jesus does not punish her or condemn her in her emotions. In fact, He joins her. Soon, He is weeping. He feels the weight of grief with His friend Martha.

And He invites her in closer to His heart, to His mission, to what it means for Him to be the Messiah. He sees her, has compassion on her, and sits in the pain with her. And then He offers faith, hope, and love to His close friend. Martha is the first to behold the truth that Jesus is the resurrection and the life and that whoever believes in Him will live. This verse has been a bedrock for our faith, and it came from an exchange with a grieving woman.

We might need to reframe the Martha we grew up with.

After this tender moment, Martha went to get her sister Mary. Mary got up, found Jesus, and in her exhaustion, worship, grief, and feelings, she fell at his feet and wept. And then Jesus wept, too.

What a gift to be able to pull back the curtain on this story and see the heightened emotional state of all their hearts. These friends were grieving together. Jesus wept with those who wept. Jesus wept with women. He taught women, He spent time with women, He comforted women, He loved women, He offered comforting words about Himself to women, and He healed women. And we know that when we watch Jesus, we see the Father. Jesus is the Father's heartbeat in the flesh. Or as Paul puts it, Jesus is "the image of the invisible God" (Colossians 1:15).

Martha and Mary show us the depth of the Father's heart for His daughters, for you. He is tender, compassionate, and comforting to them—and to you. He gives grace and truth and pulls them close to His heart—and He does the same for you.

Martha has often been typecast as a fretful, worldly busybody who is not concerned with spiritual matters. This simply is not the case. Certainly she wrestled with worry, but show me a disciple who didn't worry and I'll send you a thousand dollars. Humans worry; it's part of being human. But it's clear Martha is more than her worries. And so are you.

If you lean toward anxiety, like I do, I have found great comfort in seeing that Martha isn't just a flat character with worry as her legacy. She isn't purely emotional, with no ability to think strategically. She is layered and complex. And so are you.

And my favorite gift in seeing another side of Martha? She shows us you don't have to stay stuck underneath a label. You don't have to play the role of a worrier, a busybody, or a fretful woman. That's not the whole of who you are. A daughter is a whole, dynamic, layered, complex woman. You can choose a different story. You get to be a multifaceted human. And so does Martha.

Perhaps we can give the "worrying Martha" a second look.

Martha was in the kitchen, chopping, tasting, stirring. A masterful cook, she knew just the right amount of spice to add and not blow the heads off her guests. Which would be bad. Dinner would be served soon enough, but man, she could use some extra hands around here. Where was her sister?

She glanced out to the living room and saw Jesus teaching. But where was Mary?

There, sitting down among the men, was Mary. She was leaning on every word. Mary had always been a quick learner and took every opportunity she could to find education.

Mary had been in the kitchen earlier, but at some point she had slipped away. She was drawn by the teacher's presence. As she sat down with the disciples, she became one of them. A learner. An apprentice. A follower. Cross-legged, she crossed the boundaries of social norms and gender expectations. And she was fully welcomed to do so by Jesus Himself.

N. T. Wright shares helpful context on this scene:

Jesus declares that she is right to do so. She is "sitting at his feet"; a phrase which doesn't mean what it would mean today, the adoring student gazing up in admiration and love at the wonderful teacher. As is clear from the use of the phrase elsewhere in the NT (for instance, Paul with Gamaliel), to sit at the teacher's feet is a way of saying you are being a *student*, picking up the teacher's wisdom and learning; and in that very practical world you wouldn't do this just for the sake of informing your own mind and heart, but in order to be a teacher, a rabbi, yourself.[1]

But Martha, frustrated and fretting—quite possibly over the fact that Mary was sitting with the men—was anxious. Mary wasn't supposed to be with them. What was she doing? And in Martha's moment of overwhelm, she went straight to Jesus.

"Lord, don't you care that my sister has left me to do the work by myself? Tell her to help me!" (Luke 10:40). *Jesus, don't you care?* Her honesty is refreshing. She is overwhelmed and worried and frustrated. Her plate is too full. This is too much. She can't do it anymore. Her sister shouldn't be sitting with the men. So she says what's on her mind.

Can you just see Jesus's face right now? He looks at her with love, feels all of her overwhelm with her, and responds with a compassionate smile by saying her name.

Twice.

> "Martha, Martha," the Lord answered, "you are worried and upset about many things, but few things are needed—or indeed only one. Mary has chosen what is better, and it will not be taken away from her."
>
> Luke 10:41–42

I love what Lucy Peppiatt shows us:

> There are only seven times in the Bible when God uses a name twice—and they are all profoundly significant moments of calling: Abraham (Genesis 22:11), Jacob (Genesis 46:2), Moses (Exodus 3:4), Samuel (1 Samuel 3:10), Martha (Luke 10:41), Simon (Luke 22:31) and Saul (Acts 9:4). Martha is the only woman in the list. I believe she held a special place in Jesus' life and he knew her potential. This story is not about two sisters having an argument, but about Jesus empowering women and calling them to follow him, pointing out that agitation and anxiety will only get in the way. Its message still applies to all his disciples 2,000 years later.[2]

When a name is called twice, it is a profound moment of calling.

A profound moment of calling? I have only ever imagined the call "Martha, Martha" as a bit patronizing. The way a dad might pat a frustrated four-year-old child on the head. "Silly, Martha. You're worrying about dinner, and Mary is worrying about the kingdom of God."

But Jesus cared about every kind of bread, both spiritual and physical. He also made sure hungry people had dinner (see Luke 9:13). This wasn't about a sacred-secular divide—as if Martha only cared about domestic affairs over spiritual matters. This was Jesus interrupting some old thinking, some old wineskins, if you will. He was interrupting anxiety about dinner. He was interrupting concern about crossing cultural boundaries. He was interrupting the "this is how it's always been and should be" traditions. And He interrupted it all with a call to Himself. Something we all need every day. In this moment, both Martha and Mary are disciples. They are listening to Jesus. They are being called by Him. They are being taught by Jesus. But Jesus doesn't treat them the same; He treats them according to their need in the moment. Martha is called and Mary is confirmed. He is working in both women's lives to soften and encourage their hearts to come to Him and to know more of Him.

Because you are God's daughter, you are a disciple. And you come from a long line of disciples going back to the time of Jesus's ministry. Richard Bauckman points out how Luke's Gospel confirms this:

> In Luke's account of the visit of the women to the empty tomb of Jesus, the two angels they encounter there call on them to "remember how he told you, while he was still in Galilee, that the Son of Man must be handed over to sinners, and be crucified, and on the third day rise again" (24:6–7). These words take for granted that these women had been

in the audience of Jesus' private teaching to his disciples in Galilee.[3]

They were invited to learn from, to travel with, and to become disciples of Jesus. Jesus has been widening the table, inviting the women, the outcasts, the Gentiles, the sick, the despised, the dirty, and the outsiders since the day He arrived. You're invited, too.

You are invited to get as close to Jesus as Mary and Martha were. To learn from, to travel with, to be with Jesus, and to become like Him. You are invited to be His disciple. You have the same access these women did—women who were invited in to hear Jesus's heart. They are not more special or gifted or spiritual than you are. I am certain God is calling you closer to Him. To run to Him with your fears, to tell Him how you really feel (He knows anyway), and to learn from Him. Let these sisters encourage you to press in at His feet and to run to Him with your cries. He is here for it all. He is not bothered by your questions or your tears. He made you with layers upon layers and loves them all.

15

The First

We Are Called Upon

> "Mary!" Jesus said. She turned to him and cried out, "Rabboni!" (which is Hebrew for "Teacher").
>
> John 20:16 NLT

"You've got this, Babydoll."

My dad has always called my sister and me really affectionate names like Sweetheart and Babydoll and Doodles. He still does. I'm forty-five.

I used to be embarrassed by this during the years when, well, pretty much everything was embarrassing. Even the things I thought were not, when I look back now, well, they should have been. Like my regular outfit of hospital scrubs as pants and blue suede clogs for shoes in high school. No, I was not an ER nurse, but apparently I posed as one. God bless High School Amy.

All to say, there's no one else who says my name like my dad. Something about his voice. Which is what I love about this moment right here.

Both men went home, but she stayed. She always stayed. To clear tables, to clean up messes, to restore order to chaos, to keep it all together.

But this time, there was no keeping it together. She unraveled, openly wept. Her tears were her lament, the way crushed olives sing themselves into the finest oil.

Early morning rays glanced off dewy grass, casting a shimmery glow on the ground. The wet garden welcomed her tears in, as if they already belonged. The trees bent low, paying their respect to the sound of a daughter in distress. They had watched over graves like this for hundreds of years; they had made space for the heartbreak of loved ones lost. She had started the morning alone, and she would end it alone.

Except, there was the gardener.

How long had he been there?

Does he know anything?

Did he take the body?

He slowly walked over and stood, strong and kind, in front of her and tenderly asked, "Oh, ma'am, why are you crying? Who are you looking for?"

"Sir, if you took Him somewhere, can you tell me where? I will take it from here."

"Mary!"

And then He said her name. It caught her breath, stopped her heart. Was that her own name out of her own Creator's mouth?

And everything changed.

The minute a grave became a garden, nothing stayed the same. This was the inauguration of something entirely new, where death can no longer hold a King down. And the first order of business? A weepy woman was sent to tell the good news to the men who had all gone home.

This was a scandal within a scandal. A resurrected Jesus sent a teary woman to tell the world about it all.

It wasn't an accident Mary stayed. It wasn't a coincidence she was commissioned. It wasn't an afterthought that Jesus had a holy errand for a woman that very first new day. He was doing something new, starting in this garden.

Nothing God does is accidental.

It was no accident a few years before this when Jesus, tired as He was from traveling, sat down at a well. Long before time began, Jesus had arranged for a private conversation with a foreign woman at lunchtime.

A woman who every Jew would gladly take three days to avoid. Because, Samaria.

Samaria was often sidestepped by traveling Jews because of racist views toward their region. No one wanted to interact with Samaritans; no one wanted to go near them. Samaritans were a culture that had a mixture of both Greek and Jewish heritage, and purely Jewish folk didn't like their kind.

But then, there was Jesus.

The first person Jesus chose to reveal Himself as Messiah to was a scorned Samaritan woman. Many have added that she was sexually immoral because of what Jesus shared He knew of her story—He brings up that she has had five husbands and the man she was with was not her husband. She was a woman, some would speculate, who came to draw water at the hottest part of the day to avoid any shaming conversations because of her sinful lifestyle.

But what if there's more to the story?

Perhaps she has been unnecessarily villainized. Jesus doesn't ever tell her to "go and sin no more" the way He did with the woman who was caught in adultery. Instead, He engaged with her theological questions. Lynn Cohick writes, "It's unlikely that she was divorced five times. . . . It is more likely that her five marriages and current arrangement were the result of unfortunate events that took the lives of several of her husbands."[1] Jesus, revealing her current life and history, most likely was saying He knew her, the way He knew things about Nathanael. As well, her entire town listened to her testimony. If she was a shunned sinner, she would have been dismissed as a credible witness, but they believed her.[2] John 4:39 (NASB) says that "from that city many of the Samaritans believed in Him because of the word of the woman who testified, 'He told me all the things that I have done.'"

Perhaps the writer, John, was doing something bigger with this woman and this narrative. The story that comes before the Samaritan woman is a conversation with Nicodemus. The story of Nicodemus and the Samaritan woman are back-to-back in the book of John. But they are night and day. Literally. And on purpose.

In John 3, Nicodemus came to Jesus as a named man, a Jewish Pharisee, in a position of power, at night, as a "teacher of Israel." His dialogue decreases the longer he is with Jesus, and the metaphor they talk about is new birth, ending in confusion from Nicodemus. And then we turn the page in John 4 and find an unnamed woman, a Samaritan, who is powerless, comes at midday, and is uneducated. They have equal and shared dialogue, the metaphor they discuss is living water, and this conversation ends with recognition and a testimony that changes a town.[3]

God is always doing something bigger. Something more glorious, more grand, more welcoming, more widening than we tend to see at first glance. Which was the plan all along—Jesus coming to open up the kingdom of heaven to everyone. For both Greek and Jew, slave and free, male and female. And not to mention that this conversation took place at Jacob's well, near the same place where another daughter, named Dinah, had been violated in Genesis 34. But as Kat Armstrong points out in her book *The In-Between Place*, by coming to this well once again, Jesus is redeeming centuries of pain between Jacob's daughter Dinah and the Samaritan woman.[4]

God's redemptive plan and purposes never cease to amaze me.

The Samaritan woman left her empty water jar, filled up with truth herself. She had encountered *the* Living Water, who was for everyone. Samaria included.

The Samaritan woman was the first person Jesus revealed Himself to on His mission. She has the longest recorded dialogue with Jesus of anyone. She was the first missionary before the resurrection. And Mary was the first missionary after the resurrection. Both women. Intentionally sought out by God. Specifically set aside to go and tell.

And both of their testimonies? Changed lives.

People believed a woman's testimony about the Messiah's coming.

This is what happens when daughters are called.

Lives change.

God is glorified.

Towns are set free.

The scared are made bold.

The doubters become believers.

The world thrives.

Maybe in your context, you are not seeing other women do what is in your heart to do—maybe you are the first.

Maybe you know God has called you to go, to try, to speak, to pray, to lead, to serve, to write, to prophesy, to weep, to go on a holy errand in the middle of your everyday life for His kingdom.

You are not alone.

God has been calling His daughters from the beginning of time. He has been listening to the cry of women, He has been healing the outcast women, He has been commissioning women to join His kingdom since He made women equally in His image in that glorious first garden.

And He calls some to go first.

Here's the grand beauty of being sent with good news on behalf of the King. This is not about you; this doesn't rest on you. This is about the King and His kingdom. It is His good news, it is His glorious throne, it is His mission you join Him on. Nothing rests on your shoulders except the Father's robe of righteousness He draped upon you.

The story is still about Him. And that might be the best news of all. Whatever order we go, we go by the King's orders.

16

The Fellow Workers

We Are Honored

> I commend to you our sister Phoebe, a deacon of the church in Cenchreae. I ask you to receive her in the Lord in a way worthy of his people and to give her any help she may need from you, for she has been the benefactor of many people, including me.
>
> Romans 16:1–2

I have had a complicated relationship with the apostle Paul for quite some time. Some of the passages I read in the Bible that he wrote always read to me as confusing and frustrating and often . . . chauvinistic (can I say that?). But God clearly met him, changed his life, and then chose him to pen so many letters to the churches. Again, I've had questions. How do I reconcile his style of writing, his content, what his letters meant then, and how to apply them today?

I am happy to report that so much has become clearer over the last few years. Through studying, reading, and some of my seminary classes, I am now understanding the context of Paul's letters, the Greek gods and goddesses that were being worshiped and how he was addressing these matters, and even the fact that philosophers in the day regularly played "the boasting game." So when Paul is boasting in his letters (but about his weaknesses, not strength, and about God, not any other gods), he is writing in a way that would have been recognized by his contemporaries. Thank you, Dr. Joey Dodson, for teaching me. This hasn't cleared up every question I have, but many of my very big confusing ones. Daughter, if you have wrestled with Paul, I absolutely know that feeling. I know the confusion, the wrestling, the pesky modern-day lens we have that keeps conflicting with the real people, places, and problems that Paul was addressing in the first century. Which is why this chapter is meaningful to me. So grab my hand, and let's see what we can find together.

As Paul was closing his letter, the candle flickered. He had been writing for a long time and had lost track of it. Soon he would need someone to represent him and this letter to the growing house churches in Rome. He had gained an entire family of believers, fellow brothers and sisters in the Lord, and so many had been with him on mission. So many had risked their lives with him, had been in prison with him, and had suffered next to him. Their faith inspired him, their commitment to one another was admirable, and their love of Jesus was unrivaled. Which one should be in charge of the letter? The more he thought about it, the more he knew exactly who was the one for the job.

Phoebe.

———

Phoebe had grown up listening to her dad talk business at the dinner table. He was highly respected in the market square and was a man of great character. Everywhere they went, people stopped to talk with him, to ask a word of advice, or to say hello. As she began to mature, so did her love for business and entrepreneurship, and she soon realized she had a natural bent toward the market square herself.

In their coastal hometown of Cenchreae, she began to apply as much wisdom from her dad as she could as she began to make her own business decisions on every kind of color and cloth and fabric. And before she knew it, her own business grew. She was winsome in her business dealings in the market square. Respected by all, people also took note of how she lived her life. A woman of character and integrity, she also was smart as a whip, with a killer smile. No wonder she had influence and high status.

But once Phoebe met Jesus, she was immediately captivated by His kingdom. And just like the upside-down nature of the kingdom of God, Phoebe no longer used her reputation just for her own status or business profits. She used it to further the gospel. Her reputation and status became an asset to build the kingdom, and she became a guardian and protector of Paul and the gospel. Whatever resources and influence she had were no longer hers. Everything she had was God's. Whatever door God opened for her, she brought as many folks through it with her as she could. She used her influence to bless fellow believers, and it was something Paul was deeply thankful for.[1]

Hosting new believers to break bread and hear Paul teach, Phoebe provided a comfortable place for many to stay. After she took care of her business affairs, she would run errands and secure provisions for other believers. It wasn't just her status they were thankful for—it was the state of her heart. She was good-natured and kind, and people enjoyed her presence. They lingered at her table, and folks laughed and played easily, musing and marveling at all God was doing.

Not only was her hospitality generous, so were her financial gifts. They were indispensable to Paul, his ministry, and to the furthering of the gospel. As Paul considered his dear friend, his hand was getting tired, but his heart was far from it. Paul wanted to ensure his sister—his fellow companion in ministry—was welcomed, was provided for, and was helped in any way possible.

Paul made sure the ezers were helped, starting with Phoebe.

Since there were about six churches in Rome,[2] Phoebe had her work cut out for her. She would be traveling with this precious letter and reading, explaining, and discussing these thoughts at least six times. What a dream! As a businesswoman, she loved to travel, and she loved entrepreneurial opportunities. This was one of them. But the profit wasn't financial gain, it was spiritual multiplication. The good news of Jesus, the declaration that there is now no condemnation, the gift and inheritance of the Spirit of God, all along with the rich security of never, ever being able to be separated from her Savior's love. What a privilege she had in bringing this correspondence to the believers around the city. She and Paul had discussed these themes at length, and she understood this monumental letter.

Paul trusted her. And off she went.

When Beth Allison Barr, professor of history and associate dean of graduate studies at Baylor University with a PhD in medieval history from UNC Chapel Hill, asked a student in her class to open up their Bible to Romans 16 and record every female name Paul writes out in gratitude to close his letter, she opened up a whole world.[3] This was an exercise no one in her class had ever taken the time to do.

I used to skim the lists of names, the genealogies, anything that seemed rather stale. The end of this letter looked more like a detailed grocery list: The canned beans are in aisle 6, the best watermelon is at the bottom of the bin, and please get *unsalted* butter. Paul's salutations at the end of letters seemed to be more housekeeping with a random list of names no one ever references. Blah blah blah, get on to the action. But what I would have given to be sitting in Beth Allison Barr's class that day.

They found ten women. Paul honored ten women in the last chapter for their ministry and their faithfulness and their hard work in the gospel. Here's the list Barr's class found, along with what Barr notes about each:

> Phoebe, the deacon who carried the letter from Paul and read it aloud to her house church.
>
> Prisca (Priscilla), whose name is mentioned before her husband's name (something rather notable in the Roman world) as a coworker with Paul.
>
> Mary, a hard worker for the gospel in Asia.
>
> Junia, prominent among the apostles.
>
> Tryphaena and Tryphosa, Paul's fellow workers in the Lord.
>
> The beloved Persis, who also worked hard for the Lord.
>
> Rufus's mother, Julia, and Nereus's sister.[4]

These ten women were fellow workers, co-laborers who Paul specifically honored for their ministry service. In Romans 16, Paul writes that some "were in Christ before I was" (v. 7), they "worked very hard" (v. 6), they were "chosen in the Lord" (v. 13), they were "sisters" (vv. 1, 14, 15, 17), they were his "dear friends" (v. 12), they were "in prison with me" (v. 7), they "risked their lives for me" (v. 4), and they were "a mother to me" (v. 13). These daughters weren't messing around. They were full of faith, tenacity, strength, and diligence. He also named people from a variety of socioeconomic statuses, ranging from those who were former slaves and those who were free. In doing so, he was most likely highlighting the good news that all are equal in the kingdom of God. What a record we have in this last chapter. Twenty-nine people are named (with two names that could be assigned to either gender), and ten of those are women.[5] All to say, women were important, honored, empowered, and beloved by Paul.

Phoebe is named first in Romans 16 with significant honor and instructions for welcoming her. The more I read about Phoebe, the more I realize that the women who have gone after her have stood on her shoulders. If you have a business-minded heart and follow Jesus, Phoebe is your jam. If you have an entrepreneurial wiring but didn't think it was spiritual, be encouraged by Phoebe. If you have influence and resources and want to be more generous, be inspired by Phoebe.

Phoebe was a woman I had skimmed over in the last chapter of Paul's greatest theological letter. I had missed so much about this beloved daughter. But several scholars have slowed down and have taken note of her. And I love what they've found.

Megan Briggs gives this summary of an interview with N. T. Wright by host Jason Daye of the ChurchLeaders podcast:

> N. T. Wright says the letter to the Romans is "probably the most important letter ever written." The fact that Paul entrusted this most important letter to Phoebe, who was a deacon in the church in Corinth, is very significant when

considering the context of the time period and culture. "In the ancient world, the person who delivers the letter is the person who will read it out." . . . Additionally, there is a high possibility that Phoebe also explained Paul's meaning when people had questions about the letter. In fact, it is "highly likely the first ever exposition of Paul's letter to the Romans was done by a Christian business woman from the eastern port of Corinth," Wright said. "Paul could easily have chosen some man to do that job," he explained. Instead, he deliberately chose Phoebe.[6]

Scot McKnight confirms this:

> Since couriers were charged with taking responsibility for their letters, Phoebe probably read (performed is a better word) the letter aloud and answered questions the Roman Christians may have had. (If today's Christians, who struggle to make sense of this dense treatise called Romans, are any indication, then Phoebe may have spent days explaining this letter to the Roman churches.) Phoebe, to put this graphically, can be seen as the first "commentator" on the letter to the Romans.[7]

Nijay Gupta adds, "Paul would have had many colleagues to choose from who could have gone with or instead of Phoebe. . . . But Paul chose Phoebe to safeguard his ministry in Rome, to serve as an apostolic proxy."[8]

And finally, in an interview on *Kingdom Roots with Scot McKnight*, Lisa Bowens shared this in summarizing Zilpha Elaw's choice to continue preaching in the 1800s despite those who tried to use Paul's teachings to silence her:

> There's no way Phoebe, as a deaconess, is doing the mission of the church in silence. There's no way that's happening,

right? And [Zilpha's] talking about all these other women who are in ministry with Paul and that they are not doing this ministry in silence. And so she makes that analogy to her own ministry. As these women were not silent, so I'm not going to be silent.[9]

Phoebe was a gift to Paul, to the church, to the mission, to us. She traveled, gave generously, was well-known in the budding church, was trusted by Paul, and carried the letter to the Romans, not only reading it but explaining it. And though she has the most airtime at the top of this last chapter, Paul took the time to name nine other women. Three of the nine I want to highlight.

Junia, for quite some time, was translated as Junias, a male. But Michael F. Bird states that "there is a tsunami of textual and patristic evidence for 'Junia' that proves overwhelming. Despite some naughty scribes, biased translators, lazy lexicographers, and dogmatic commentators, the text speaks about a woman named 'Junia.'"[10] It's clear Paul has great respect for Adronicus and Junia, whom he describes as "my fellow Jews who have been in prison with me," "outstanding among the apostles," and "in Christ before I was" (Romans 16:7).

Prisca (Priscilla) and Aquila were a married couple named in six passages in the New Testament (Acts 18:2, Acts 18:18–19, Acts 18:26, Romans 16:3, 1 Corinthians 16:19, and 2 Timothy 4:19). In four out of the six times, Priscilla's name is listed before her husband's name, Aquila, which may have meant she held a higher status than he did, in contrast to the usual custom of naming the husband first. Lynn H. Cohick writes, "The name order might also signal Priscilla's superior teaching capabilities, for when Acts 18:26 notes that the couple taught Apollos, her name appears first."[11] Paul says that all the churches of the Gentiles are grateful for Priscilla and Aquila and commends them for risking their lives for him! Paul has a high respect for Priscilla and Aquila and has no issue naming her first.

And toward the end of Paul's greetings, he greets Rufus and his mother. He doesn't call her by name, but as we know, the nameless women have been the unseen backbone to many situations in Scripture. What we do see is the fond affection Paul has for Rufus's mother. He says she "has been a mother to me, too" (Romans 16:13). She mattered to him. Being included and being loved by other mothers in our lives makes a difference. How many bonus mothers have given us advice, hugged us, listened to us, opened their homes to us, fed us, and been present to our problems? We don't have much detail in the passage except that she was a mother to him, too. Did she make sure Paul had plenty of food? Did she fuss over Paul's wardrobe and patch up his pants? Did she pray over him for protection? Whatever her mothering looked like, in all the possible shapes and sizes, Paul felt loved and wanted to make sure Rufus passed on to his own mother a solid and warm greeting.

From a businesswoman who traveled as his stand-in representative to an unnamed mother, Paul commended every kind of work, inside the home and outside of it. Because it all matters. The fact that Paul included Rufus's mother—making note of her motherhood toward him—is such a sweet and softhearted gesture. One we don't want to take lightly from a former seething persecutor of those who followed Jesus.

This meticulous list is for honoring the women whose shoulders we stand upon, the many daughters who worked as co-laborers with Paul (and there are other women named in other letters!). This list is for those of us who may have had a hard time with Paul, wondering if he was really cheering on women in light of certain passages taught by certain folks. This is to redeem what we may have thought was true about women in ministry, and to see the vital importance of brothers and sisters serving side by side. Not one without the other but the clear need for both to be working together on this glorious gospel project. This is to redeem any notion that women didn't travel or teach or interpret Scripture or risk their lives for the gospel or mother unto the kingdom of God. They most certainly did. This list is to agree with Gupta's words about women: "The story of Jesus can't be told without them."[12]

17

The Single Women

We Are Family

Therefore go and make disciples of all nations, baptizing them in the name of the Father and of the Son and of the Holy Spirit, and teaching them to obey everything I have commanded you. And surely I am with you always, to the very end of the age.

Matthew 28:19–20

As we just looked at Paul's greetings to end his letter to the churches in Rome, Phoebe was a major player. And she is highlighted by herself, not next to a husband or even in a ministry pair (as some spouses, some women, and some mother-son duos are paired). Many scholars believe Phoebe was single or perhaps widowed. It's clear throughout Scripture that God has good work to do for every daughter, in each season of life, whether single, married, divorced, or widowed. Jesus Himself healed, commissioned, protected, defended, and honored single women. Such heroes of the faith were single women in some of the significant moments when they acted out their faith and were recognized by God for it: Esther, Rahab, Mary Magdalene, Ruth and Naomi, Anna, Martha, Dorcas, Lydia, and Phoebe, to name a few.

And of course, we serve a Messiah who was single. As was Paul.

But author and Bible teacher (and single female at the time of this writing) Tara-Leigh Cobble notes when it comes to singleness, "The messaging of the church has been inconsistent with the messaging of Scripture."[1]

How so?

Yes, the first couple in the garden of Eden was called to be fruitful and multiply and fill the earth. And then when they were banished from the garden, having children was going to bring the one who would crush the head of Satan and restore everything. God was going to bring restoration through a baby from a mother in a family. So creating families was quite important. But today, the commission isn't to be fruitful and multiply the earth with children, it's to be fruitful and multiply the earth with disciples. Which anyone can do, married or not. Leaving this earth, Jesus left us with this Great Commission to go and make disciples of all nations, baptizing them and teaching them everything about Jesus. Marriage not required. A. J. Swoboda states, "Who is the most fruitful person in human history? Jesus is, and he never has sex. Fruitfulness is not the result of sexual union. It is a part of it, it can be, but it's not the whole kit and caboodle."[2]

God created humanity in the beginning. He created humans as a species to be male and female. And in the second chapter of Genesis, God says that it's not good for man to be alone. Carolyn Custis James writes,

This powerful statement indicates the fact that men and women need each other. God doesn't narrow the parameters of his statement to marriage, the home, the church, any other sphere. It is a blanket statement encompassing every arena of life. Something serious is missing if men operate in any venue without partnering with women. This sheds a glaring light on how the marginalization and oppression of women is not only disastrous for women, but also for men.[3]

This is where being brothers and sisters in Christ is paramount. God is our Father, and we are given a family. We are given one another as brothers and sisters to honor, celebrate, and work alongside to usher in the kingdom of God. We are better together, married or not.

I've been married for twenty-three years, so a chapter from me on being single is not exactly ideal. It hasn't been my reality or my perspective. Though I have several friends who are single, it's not my lived experience. So in my research and studying, I wanted the voices of women who love Jesus, who are living in a church community, and who are currently single to be heard. And I could think of no one better than my seminary sisters at Denver Seminary to ask. These women in my cohort come from different cities, backgrounds, ethnicities, and perspectives. I asked four of them to write their thoughts on singleness and what they wished the church today would know about being single.

"In my years in the church, I've cherished my sense of belonging, yet I've observed a notable oversight in how the church engages with single adults. Despite the church being a beacon of joy and community, moments have arisen when I've felt marginalized due to a prevailing focus on family-centric programming, which tends to sideline singles. My experiences have led me to view singleness not as a lesser state but as a significant calling to live out Christ's love, unrestricted by marital status. What the church needs to understand about singleness is that, though I am open to marriage, I find completeness in Christ and lead a fulfilling life. As I embrace aging, I've perceived an inclination within the church to phase out my generation in favor of younger members. However, I believe that some of my best days lie ahead. The blend of wisdom and experience with the vigor and fresh ideas of youth creates a powerful synergy. Moreover, as an African American woman, I see it as part of my mission to connect different cultures and generations—a task I am fully equipped to undertake as a single individual."

Cheryl Luke, founder, The Mosaic Life

"I love the Church. I can never remember a time in my life when I didn't love the Church. I loved her when I was seven years old, playing tag with my friends after Wednesday night fellowship hall, in middle school and awkward "special youth night" performances, straight through college and into full-time ministry, where I currently serve as a teaching pastor. I love her. Always have. Always will. But somewhere along the way, the love of a spouse became the equivalent of love with God, an idolatry that can slither in faster than "I do."

The truth? I don't think the Church meant to forget us. (Singles, I mean.) I don't think anyone set out to create an environment where marriage was as paramount as salvation, where single men and women above the age of twenty-five were seen as running out of time and "probably just too picky," or where singleness was reduced to a "season of waiting" (as if singleness communicated a life on hold). But that is sure what it started to feel (and sound) like. I heard messages where Scripture was used to prove that "marriage is the greatest display of the gospel this side of eternity." Sometimes, if not very often, the Church made me feel like I was on "the B team," waiting to be called up to the big leagues of marriage. Until then, all I needed to do was prepare. As if preparing to become a "good gift" would finally make me valuable enough to become a wife. Again, no one wanted anything but the absolute best for me and friends like me! However, when marriage is consistently referred to as the height of calling and singleness simply the means of preparation to get there, then marriage becomes the goal other than Christ. And let me tell ya, when the clouds part and the trumpet sounds and the shining face of Glory Himself is finally in full view, every "I do" will find its fulfillment in Him and Him alone—our ultimate bridegroom, our final wedding. Single or married, this is the goal. Marriage may be a great gift, but it ain't the ultimate one. He is.

Marriage is a calling, not a command. "Now as a concession, not a command, I say this. I wish that all were as I myself am. But each has his own gift from God, one of one kind and one of another" (1 Corinthians 7:6–7 ESV).

Paul talks about marriage and singleness as if they are on the same playing field. Each a calling. Each a gift. Similarly, the Old Testament command to "be fruitful and multiply" is no longer confined to the reproduction of biological children. We are under a New Covenant. We live within a new definition of family, where Christ is our big brother, uniting us to the Father and calling us to "go and make disciples." The Church of Jesus Christ is truly living within its purpose when the people of God are multiplying disciples, not just babies. We are truly alive when there are more baptisms than weddings. More confession and repentance than vows and dance floors. More unity in the Spirit than unifying of last names.

To continue to heighten marriage above singleness is to step outside of biblical bounds. If we continue to idolize marriage, we continue to encourage singles to pursue dating and marriage above simple delight in obedience to God. I have never known a love like Jesus. And whether I ever get married or not, I will be a better single person, a better wife, and a better woman because I have already found the love of my life in Christ alone. Marriage is such a beautiful gift. But it is not a better one. When single and married people alike understand this, we will love more freely, more fully, and more spiritually.

Lastly, Jesus was single. If marriage is the greatest display of the gospel on this side of eternity, what do we do with Jesus?"

Meredith Knox, teaching pastor, NewSpring Church

"The experiences that I've had in the African-American church are very different from my experiences in white churches because there wasn't this emphasis on marriage. There's an interdependence and a very collective nature in this space. There was a confidence and courage that I had as I saw other people in my situation as an older single woman. My friend circle was very diverse in the sense of having friends that were married and married with children and they were very inclusive of me and their life. I never felt on the outskirts. I wasn't a unicorn.

I never felt more single than in the white church. It was a new thing because mostly everyone was married and had gotten married really young; that is not the case in the African-American community. Even the women's ministry was centered around motherhood and being a wife, which didn't speak to me or my life.

The church needs to do a better job at seeing older single women. The community can look different, small groups can look different, more integration to all the factors of single-hood could look different. Also, some churches won't hire single leaders, which doesn't make sense; Jesus was single. Singleness shouldn't dictate our leadership ability or the call on our life."

Latasha Morrison, speaker and author of
Be the Bridge and *Brown Faces, White Spaces*

———

"Being a single woman in ministry often brings a sense of isolation, especially within the church, where the emphasis frequently leans toward preparing for marriage rather than equipping us to navigate singleness. It's challenging to find examples or guidance on how to value this phase of life. My quest to understand how to meaningfully live as a single person in ministry often hits a wall, lacking a clear model or advice. Yet, through this solitude, I've discovered that God entrusted me with this path not only for my growth but also to demonstrate to other single women that it's perfectly fine to thrive during this time. Paul speaks to the beauty of singleness, highlighting it as a time of undivided devotion to God. This season allows me to pursue God wholeheartedly, free from the responsibilities toward a spouse and children. While I anticipate the joys of family life, I'm currently embracing the opportunity to deepen my relationship with God without reservations. This period of complete surrender and enjoying my relationship with God is truly fulfilling.

I wish the church would better recognize and celebrate the blessings of singleness, reinforcing that one's ministry calling is not diminished by their marital status. Being single adds to our lives; it isn't merely a waiting period for completion. Living with intention in singleness allows us to fulfill our purpose, and when the time comes, my future husband and I will enhance each other's lives, not seeking completion."

Brenda Palmer, preacher and host of
Life in Perspective podcast

Every woman who shared her life experiences above has given me a beautiful perspective shift. I honor these women, the call God has on their lives, and the richness they each bring to the table. To the daughters reading this book who are single: You are a beautiful, necessary, and nourishing part of the body of Christ. God has good work for you to do, and there is nothing wrong with you—you are not diminished, you are not lacking. The body of Christ is depleted without you. You are the Father's daughter, and you have everything you need. You have so much to offer, so much to celebrate, so much to teach us. May God bless your life richly, may you know the depth of the Father's love as His daughter, and may you be confident in who God made you to be.

As A. J. Swoboda says, "Celibacy and singleness is not a form of Christian leprosy; it is not a signpost of failure,"[4] even if one of the sad realities of the Church is that it sometimes portrays marriage as the highest calling. I am sure I have bought into this lie and have contributed to this in some way, which grieves me. Swoboda puts it beautifully this way:

> If we are going to invite people to place their sexuality on the cross out of faithfulness to God, then we'd better be ready to make room at the dinner table for single people. And we'd better be ready to make room on our eldership teams for single people. . . . We need to be the one place in the world where somebody can feel fulfilled and be fulfilled in their singleness.[5]

As we consider our brothers and sisters who are single in the church, may our lens be one of family and our dinner tables be welcoming. In the New Testament, we read about Jesus traveling with his disciples and living life in community, staying at different houses for dinner and lodging, and creating a family of those who are with Him, following God the Father together. Some of them are married men (Peter), and some of them are married and single women (Luke 8). Jesus even challenges the idea of family when His mother and brothers come to find Him, saying, "For whoever does the will of my Father in heaven is my brother and sister and mother!" (Matthew 12:50).

Daughters in Christ, whether married or single, belong to the family of God. We belong to the Father of compassion and the God of all comfort (see 2 Corinthians 1:3). May we practice sharing bread and generosity and feeding one another with good food and story and song. May we bring the flavor of blessing and the gift of belonging. May we practice inviting others to our homes to share a box of mac and cheese and a few good questions in our pocket to stir up stories and weary souls. May we foreshadow The Great Wedding Feast in Revelation. May we create spaces for others to feel a little more at home in our world, and may we have Eden in view, where both breath and belonging fill up our lungs.

Whatever gifts we have to give, may we give them generously to one another. May we give hugs and warm affection, seats at the dinner table, and the names *aunt* and *uncle* for our kids to call our brothers and sisters in Christ. May our families be bigger than our DNA and our tables wider than our last name. We share the blood of Jesus and acknowledge His sacrifice, by which He invited all to the table.

18

The Grandmas

We Are Needed

I recall your sincere faith that first lived in your grandmother Lois and in your mother Eunice and now, I am convinced, is in you also.

2 Timothy 1:5 CSB

My big, loud, German-Czech family gatherings meant comfort food, laughter, storytelling, and children tugging on adults telling inappropriate jokes crowded next to the fridge with Coors Light in their hands. It meant blueberry cheesecake with graham cracker crust, badminton, and fart-noise contests instigated by the uncles. It meant leaving the daily grind behind for a few hours as middle-class blue-collar folks. It meant children feeling a sense of belonging in big and little ways and swells of laughter slipping their way out of an overcrowded kitchen, through the cracked window, and into the cool November night. It meant pulling in the weathered picnic table from the backyard, squeezing her through the sliding glass doors, and plopping her right into the living room. It meant adding a plastic white tablecloth to fancy her up for more seating.

And it meant my Grandma Badik, laughing in the kitchen, swatting my uncles' fingers away as they tried to taste test everything. She was always laughing, giving me little jobs to feel proud of as an eight-year-old, rolling her playful eyes at whatever ridiculousness her grandkids were up to in the front room that no one was supposed to be in with the nice furniture, the fireplace, and the record player.

There's something about grandmas. Something about that generational gap that somehow says you can do no wrong, even though her daughter did the same thing and got in trouble for it. The generations ahead of us usually have enough wisdom to give enough grace. At least in my experience.

So when Paul names Timothy's grandma, Lois, I think of my Grandma Badik, Angie. He also names Eunice, Timothy's mom, and says he is mindful of their sincere faith that dwells in them. The faith of the women who had gone before Timothy paved the way for him, who Paul affectionately calls his son in the faith and remembers in his daily prayers (see 2 Timothy 1:1–4). Paul specifically and purposefully writes that he is mindful and remembers where Timothy's faith started: dwelling inside his grandmother and mother and now him. The faith of one grandmother can pioneer the faith of the entire next generation.

It wasn't Timothy's father who shaped his faith. The first mention of Lois and Eunice tells us that Timothy's father was Greek. His grandmother and mother were Jewish believers in Jesus, but his dad was not:

Paul came to Derbe and then to Lystra, where a disciple named Timothy lived, whose mother was Jewish and a believer but whose father was a Greek. The believers at Lystra and Iconium spoke well of him. Paul wanted to take him along on the journey, so he circumcised him because of the Jews who lived in that area, for they all knew that his father was a Greek.

Acts 16:1–3

Was there a debate those first few days of Timothy's life between Eunice and her husband about circumcising him? And if there was, it looks like his father won, because Timothy wasn't circumcised. So he wasn't seen fully as a Jew. Did Eunice carry doubt, regret, fear, or shame for having a son who wasn't fully accepted by the Jewish community and also not fully accepted in the Greek community with a Jewish woman as a mom? I wonder what God did in her heart through her wrestling.

One thing we know for sure is that she kept her faith and passed it on. Scholars seem to think Timothy's father, never named, was either dead or divorced from Eunice. Which could have added to the pain Eunice felt for her son.

But the family of God can fill in the blanks of many of the aching holes in our lives. Paul steps in and becomes a father to Timothy. Paul wanted to take Timothy under his wing and take him on his travels to spread the gospel. And Paul did what a Jewish father would have done: circumcised Timothy so they could fully minister to the Jews. Not as a way to earn anything, but to be seen and accepted in the community he was ministering to.

Timothy busted through the heavy back door, the way he had for years, with adventure in his eyes. But this latest adventure was bigger than tree climbing and fishing.

"Mom, Paul wants to take me with him to strengthen and encourage the churches!"

Eunice, chopping leeks and onions, could have blamed the produce. But she would be lying. Her tears weren't about the onions. They came immediately from the excitement in her son's voice at being noticed and needed. Hearing that her son was invited by Paul—the determined tentmaker who was taking the good news of Jesus all across the region—brought the tears. Her tears came from years of heartache, wondering if her life was too messy to make a difference. Her tears came because her life had not ended up how she imagined, and she wondered if God cared or had seen or had punished her. Her tears came from some place of relief, because God had answered a decade of prayers. Or more. All she had wanted for Timothy was that he know God and follow Him wholeheartedly. She longed for wise men to see the gifts inside her son and to take him under their wing. Many mornings she had started on her knees, interceding for her half-Jew, half-Greek son to be fully captured by God's own heart.

Paul saw Timothy the way she did.

She slowly put her knife down, turned around, and took a good look at her son's face. He was not a child anymore; he was a man. And she had trusted God to raise him, and God had been doing it all along. And now Jehovah Jirah—God provides—had provided a father figure in his life.

"Timothy! Of course you must go! That's amazing."

The kitchen was full of anticipation of an adventure. But she knew her son. There was still a hesitation in his eyes. Was there a catch? Was it too good to be true? He had more to say.

"But there's one thing he said I need to do. . . ."

They both knew it. Circumcision had come up throughout his life. And Timothy was quite aware of his mixed roots: Jewish and

Greek. His Greek father had not allowed it. He wouldn't bear the mark of the Jews.

But he was a man now, and it was Timothy's choice.

"What's all the commotion around here?" asked Grandma Lois, rounding the corner carrying laundry dried by the fresh Mediterranean air. The woman rarely sat down. Timothy immediately moved to help his grandma and take some of the load out of her arms. She tried to fuss and say she had it, but Timothy had learned to fuss back. He helped wherever he could.

"Paul invited me to join him in his travels," he told his grandmother.

"Shondala!" she exclaimed and dropped the remains of the clean laundry on the floor, hands shooting up in the air in praise. She always said this when she was surprised or overwhelmed with joy. No one knew where she got it; that was just Grandma Lois.

"Oh, my grandson! What a day! You must go. God is faithful and will provide for you. The Lord is compassionate and gracious, slow to anger and abounding in loving kindness and faithfulness to us." She was always quoting Torah to him, reminding him who God said He was to Moses.

Always full of affection, they moved in for a group hug, all three of them in the kitchen. Smelling of onions, clean clothes, and sweat from tentmaking, their little family was teary and grateful for the call on Timothy's life. The call both his grandmother and mother had prayed to God to bring into fruition.

God saw and honored the faith of Lois and Eunice. Though their lives took twists and turns, their faith hung in at every curve. They were faithful with what they were handed. They didn't have a big stage, a microphone, one hundred thousand followers, or published books. They had their one life, their faith in God, their determination to put a deposit in their grandson and son. There are many faithful ways to live a life.

Paul saw what the women of faith saw, too. Timothy traveled to "Corinth, Greece, Rome, Ephesus, and Macedonia, sometimes with Paul or sometimes while waiting in a city to be summoned by Paul."[1] Timothy was well versed in sound doctrine and the Torah (no doubt because of the influence of the Jewish women in his life), but he also needed encouragement because he was young in ministry. Paul encouraged him to let no one look down on him because he was young, but in everything—"in speech, in conduct, in love, in faith and in purity"—to be an example of those who believe (1 Timothy 4:12). Which is something he certainly saw growing up. We have no Timothy if we don't have Lois. Her faith shaped his mother's life and, in turn, his life.

This one is for the daughters who are our grandmothers of faith. We need you. You hold treasures from dark valleys and scars from hard-fought battles. We need you to point us to Jesus when everything feels dim. There is no ageism with the Spirit of God. Keep pouring into us. This is for the young daughters who crave spiritual mothers and grandmothers. Find the older generation, maybe the ones who think the church doesn't need them anymore, and tell them that's hogwash and you do. You need them. I need them. We need them.

There is an entire generation of spiritual grandmothers and mothers who don't believe they have much to offer or that they don't qualify as mentors of the faith. But do you see the fruit from a life of abiding in the vine of Jesus? Do you see love, joy, peace, patience, kindness, goodness, faithfulness, gentleness, and self-control in an older woman? Then invite her over for spaghetti and garlic bread. Ask her about how God has been faithful to her. Make a list of ten things you want to know—what is one of the hardest roads she walked, and what did she learn? Where did she feel disappointed by God? Why does she still cling to Jesus? What advice does she have for you? What does her prayer life look like?

May we honor the grandmas and mothers of our faith, making sure they are a vibrant part of the family of God.

SECTION 3

RECEIVING

This section is about receiving. After the first section of belonging and the second one of healing, we move to this last section on receiving. How do you truly receive your name, daughter?

If you're anything like me, it's hard to open your hands to receive something. It's hard to come with empty hands. Your hands are used to being full and busy. I imagine your hands are resourceful as they make lunches from scraps in the fridge. Maybe your hands are calloused from physical labor, from hours working as a single mom, trying to make ends meet. Maybe your hands are tightfisted in frustration at life's circumstances right now. Maybe your hands don't know the first thing about being still or open or empty.

So this section is for you. The one with the tired hands from holding up the world. Tired of proving, pushing, producing to be called good enough. To be safe. To be seen. To be loved. This section is the opposite of earning the right to be a daughter and just about being the daughter you are. Where simply being God's beloved daughter is everything, and nothing can separate your name from your soul.

19

The Spirit-Filled Daughters

We Are Filled with God

And afterward, I will pour out my Spirit on all people. Your sons and daughters will prophesy . . .

Joel 2:28

The tears wouldn't stop. Which is interesting, because my soul had felt so dried up, so thirsty to see something like this for so long. But now fresh, salty springs poured out of my soul and down my face.

A room full of pastors, leaders, and Bible teachers who were worshiping, singing, teaching, confessing, praying, healing, prophesying, and sharing words of truth and wisdom.

And they were all women.

They were female pastors and leaders who had been seen, commissioned, called, anointed, and had stepped into their churches to shepherd. That's what it means to be a pastor—from the Latin word that means to shepherd. To oversee a flock with care.

We were at a retreat to kick off a six-month leadership cohort for women who serve in some leadership capacity as pastors, directors, church staff members, worship leaders, and volunteers in their local church.[1] And the sheer number of women who introduced themselves as *pastor* was jaw-dropping to me. And beautiful. And healing. As tears ran down my cheeks, one of my friend's words rang in my ear. To prepare me for coming, she had said to me, *"Just come and receive."*

Just receive. Receive care. Receive hope. Receive healing. Receive strength. Receive belovedness. Receive the rights and privileges and blessings of being God's daughter. Receive solid teaching. Receive hands on you in prayer. Receive beauty. Receive the power of the Spirit of God. Receive in community. Receive your name: daughter.

So often we as daughters don't know how to receive. We give and give and give. We work and push and pull and arrange and hold and share and schedule and fix and hope. But receive? That hardly crosses our minds. It's as if we need permission to simply be, with hands open. To let ourselves be loved. To open our hearts to take it all in. Which is the entire thing about being God's daughters. We are His beloved. We must practice just that: being loved. As my executive pastor often says to our staff team at church, "More being, less doing."

And so I opened my hands in worship as a symbol of just being. Of being and receiving. Of receiving the gifts of God's goodness and kindness and grace upon us. Of receiving His love and mercy and compassion. Of receiving

His calling upon me. And I let other women pastor me into this place.

For the longest time, I hadn't heard a woman called a pastor. But it was odd, because I saw women *pastoring*. I saw them caring, teaching, leading, serving, making meals, correcting, praying, providing for, and loving others. And we have seen women do this all over the Bible—caring for the flock under their own roof, shepherding those with needs outside their home, standing in the gap for others, laying their lives down for the flock in cities and homes and jail cells. Whether by title or not, women have long been shepherding others. Young and old, married or not, women have been pointing to the kingdom of God, speaking about His glory and His power. Like Anna.

Her bones ached as she got out of bed. Her bed that she had briefly shared, for seven years, as a young bride. They had seven sweet years together, her husband and her. But no children were had, no legacy was created, no heirs to honor her deceased lover.

Bitterness knocked on her door constantly. He wanted her to wallow, to sulk, to cry "why me?" Her eighty-something-year-old body was getting tired. Eighty-two? Eighty-four? She was always forgetting her age. And she couldn't remember the last time she'd had a birthday celebration. Without children to throw her parties, often the day had come and gone. She also didn't have any grandchildren running around calling her sweet names for grandma or asking for more slices of fresh honey-topped raisin cakes from her oven. She had every reason to bake up fresh batches of bitterness every morning instead.

Luke, the doctor and Gospel writer, seemed to love to hear from women and to pass on the stories he captured, and his writing includes more stories about women than any other Gospel. Anna is one of them. In Luke 2:36, he records that Anna was from the tribe of Asher. The Basilica of the National Shrine of the Immaculate Conception shares this about her:

> As a widow in Jewish society, most likely without children, she had little way to provide for herself and most likely was dependent on the charity of others to survive. . . . [Her tribe of Asher] was taken into captivity in Babylon and did not return intact, so it was unlikely that she had an extended family network to rely on.[2]

Despite these challenges, she was determined to keep her heart soft and her eyes on the coming Messiah.

Her name means *grace*, and this seemed evident—God poured grace upon her heart as she stayed in the temple, praying and fasting and waiting.[3] She chose to get up each morning, to shift her perspective, to pray *God, you are my stronghold*, as Psalm 18 declares.

And when Jesus was born, Anna was the spark that began the fulfillment of what the prophet Joel prophesied and Peter confirmed. And she was in her eighties.

Joel writes in the Old Testament that after captivity, after disaster, and after the Messiah comes,

> Then you will know that I am in Israel,
>   that I am the LORD your God,
>   and that there is no other;
> never again will my people be shamed.
> And afterward,

I will pour out my Spirit on all people.
Your sons and daughters will prophesy,
   your old men will dream dreams,
   your young men will see visions.
Even on my servants, both men and women,
   I will pour out my Spirit in those days.

Joel 2:27–29

When Jesus arrived, the Spirit poured out onto Anna and she prophesied. And her prophecy shepherded the flock around her. The Messiah's arrival started the pouring. Jesus's life and ministry were a constant pouring of the best wine out of water jugs, of a new law of love in our hearts, of compassion upon crowds of lost men and women who were hungry to be fed.

Joel said that God was going to pour out His Spirit on *all* people. And he names sons and daughters, young and old, servants, both men and women. *All* means *all*. And Anna was proof.

Can you just see her, a wooden cane in one hand, the other hand outstretched, wrinkly, and joyfully touching the cheek of the baby Messiah she had been waiting for? Can you see her holding Jesus, next to Simon in the temple, who was rejoicing over the sweetest bundle of joy? Can you see her cuddling God? I am sure Mary willingly and proudly passed her baby to Simon, who then handed him to Anna. Anna, so often overlooked, was one of the first to look at the face of God.

Simon told God, for all to hear, that he could now be dismissed in peace because his eyes had seen God's salvation—a light for the Gentiles and the glory of Israel (see Luke 2:32). Simon was pointing at the *all* of who Jesus came for. Both

Jews and Gentiles would be able to know God, to live a life with God, to have His Spirit poured out upon them.

And Anna was right there with him: "Coming up to them at that very moment, she gave thanks to God and spoke about the child to all who were looking forward to the redemption of Jerusalem" (Luke 2:38). The prophet Anna couldn't keep quiet—she spoke to everyone about who this was and the redemption of Jerusalem that had just arrived in the tiniest, helpless package of a baby boy.

Only a handful of women are named as prophets: Miriam (Exodus 15:20), Deborah (Judges 4:4), Huldah (2 Chronicles 34:22), Isaiah's wife (Isaiah 8:3), four unmarried daughters of Philip the evangelist (Acts 21:8–9), and Anna. A blip in the Christmas story. We could almost miss her. But God never misses a daughter. He pours His Spirit out on us.

Anna is the female prophet who lives in between Joel and Pentecost. In between when Joel declared the Spirit was coming for all—daughters included—and when Peter preached Joel's same words as tongues of fire danced upon their heads in those first days of the early church. She was a prophetic daughter pointing at more to come.

Daughter, you are never too young or too old to speak life, to encourage others, to hear from God, and to shepherd others. Whether you are widowed, married, single, divorced—the kingdom needs your voice, your experiences, your testimony. We need your words, your warnings, your hope. And if you feel far away from God right now, He has not left you. He is here. Ask Him to help you experience His presence. Ask Him for faith like Anna's. He delights in you and adores you.

Anna was there at Jesus's birth, and more women were there after His resurrection. After Jesus died, was buried, rose from the grave, and ascended into heaven, God did something outrageous among a group of men and women who were huddled together, praying. Don't miss who was there:

> Then the apostles returned to Jerusalem from the hill called the Mount of Olives, a Sabbath day's walk from the city. When they arrived, they went upstairs to the room where they were staying. Those present were Peter, John, James and Andrew; Philip and Thomas, Bartholomew and Matthew; James son of Alphaeus and Simon the Zealot, and Judas son of James. They all joined together constantly in prayer, along with the women and Mary the mother of Jesus, and with his brothers.
>
> Acts 1:12–14

They were all together. The eleven disciples, "along with the women and Mary the mother of Jesus." This is very reminiscent of Luke 8:1–3 when the group of women was traveling with Jesus and His disciples. What happened next wasn't reserved for just the eleven disciples. God made sure Jesus's mother was there (what a gift for her!) and more women. This was a defining moment for the start of the church, and God had specific plans for both men and women:

> When the day of Pentecost came, they were all together in one place. Suddenly a sound like the blowing of a violent wind came from heaven and filled the whole house where they were sitting. They saw what seemed to be tongues of fire that separated and came to rest on each of them. All of them were filled with the Holy Spirit and began to speak in other tongues as the Spirit enabled them.
>
> Acts 2:1–4

Wind and fire and the filling of the Holy Spirit and the languages of other nations. I told you—outrageous. Then Peter stood up in front of the crowd who had gathered and called back to Joel 2, quoting how the Spirit of God would come upon sons and daughters, young and old, servants of all kinds—male and female.

God was doing a new thing through His Holy Spirit. And it was made clear that everybody plays. Sons and daughters, Jews and Greeks, slave and free, every nation, every color, every tribe, every gender. "Each one heard their own language being spoken" (Acts 2:6). This was no longer just about Israel. This was the great pouring, this was the unbiased gift of the Spirit of God, and this was for everyone.

It's because of this story in Acts, quoting Joel, that my tears began to fall on that day. The tears came as a roomful of women leaders and pastors were worshiping and leading and praying and teaching. Because God has poured His Spirit inside anyone who believes in Him, as I had read about in Acts 2. He has given us fresh breath, fresh life-giving energy, fresh gifts to use. And Peter, quoting Joel, specifically named daughters. Specifically said both men and women. Specifically included male and female, the way Genesis 1:27 specifically says, "So God created mankind in his own image, in the image of God he created them; male and female he created them."

We both, men and women, bear God's image and we both have access to the Spirit of God and we both have a full range of gifts from that very same Spirit—gifts that are not gender specific. The gifts God gives us are not limited to one gender—Paul did not limit who could have the gifts of apostle, prophet, evangelist, shepherd, or teacher in Ephesians 4. He just said those gifts are given, hard stop (and more gifts are listed in 1 Corinthians 12–14 and Romans 12). "So Christ himself gave the apostles, the prophets, the evangelists, the pastors and teachers, to equip his people for works of service, so that the body of Christ may be built up" (Ephesians 4:11–12). We see why the gifts are given: to equip and to build up. And we also see who they are given to: to everyone.

The same tears came when I read these words from Beth Allison Barr. She wrote about the Greek word for *elder* in 1 Timothy 3:

> We assume 1 Timothy 3:1–13 is referencing men in leadership roles (overseer/bishop and deacon). But is this because of how our English Bibles translate the text? Whereas the Greek text uses the words *whoever* and *anyone*, with the only specific reference to *man* appearing in verse 12 (a literal Greek translation of the phrase is "one woman man," referencing the married state of deacons), modern English Bibles have introduced eight to ten male pronouns within the verses. None of those male pronouns in our English Bibles are in the Greek text. [Lucy] Peppiatt concludes that the problem with female leadership is not actually the biblical text; it is the "relentless and dominant narrative of male bias" in translations.[4]

The idea of a male bias when it came to the word *elder* in some Bible translations stopped me in my tracks. Wait, what? The questions came as the tears fell. My tears were prompted by a mixed bag of curiosity, defensiveness, fear, holy trepidation, and validation. And I know, friend, this idea might really ruffle some feathers. Different ideas can do that to us. But Barr's words spoke to something I had been wondering about for a while. So it was time to do some digging for myself. I started to study, read, and ask the Spirit to help me understand. What was long-held tradition? What was the original Greek? What translations said what? What was God saying in not just a few places in Scripture but from Genesis to Revelation? What were scholars saying across the spectrum on women in leadership? What was I afraid of and why? Friend, your curiosity and your questions matter. I've included a Resources page at the back of this book with some of the resources that helped me answer so many of my questions. May you feel free to ask your questions, to explore, to learn, to dig, to take your time, to sit at the feet of Jesus, and to listen to Him. May you embrace the messy middle of exploration with those who welcome the wrestling. Jesus asked more than three hundred questions, so you're in good company. Hebrews 12:28 says God's kingdom is unshakable, which includes your curiosity. Curiosity can't shake the kingdom of God—and in fact, it often builds it.

Here's what I know for certain from that monumental day at Pentecost: The Spirit came powerfully on both men and women when the church began. "I will pour out my Spirit on all people" (Joel 2:28). No longer just priests or Levites or Moses or Isaiah or Israelites or kings. As author and pastor Tara Beth Leach says to women often, "The Kingdom of God flourishes when all voices are heard. Your teaching, preaching, and leadership embody the in-breaking power of God's Kingdom, inviting all to the table."[5] The Spirit is here for the rest of the tribes, the mothers and daughters and granddaughters, the servants, the bordering nations, the young, the old, the named and unnamed, the married and the single, the queens and the tentmakers, the abandoned, the marginalized, the abused, the rich, the light skinned, the dark skinned, the ones with leprous skin, the Gentiles.

All means all. Daughter, you are invited to the Spirit-filled, empowered, gift-giving life. You are the Father's precious one whom He loves, fills, sends, equips, and empowers by His Holy Spirit. When you see Mary and the women there that wild and beautiful day, may it give you a fuller picture of the kingdom of Heaven.

20

The Daughters of Job

We Have an Inheritance

A woman should learn in quietness and full submission.
I do not permit a woman to teach or to assume authority
over a man; she must be quiet. For Adam was formed first,
then Eve.

1 Timothy 2:11–13

The first day of my second semester in seminary, our professor, Dr. Judith Diehl, taught us a big fancy phrase that we asked no less than sixty-seven times how to spell.

Hapax legomenon.

The group chat went nuts.

"What did she just say?"

"Was she speaking in tongues?"

"Did anyone catch that?"

"Was that a sneeze?!"

"All I heard was 'mah na mah na' from the Muppets . . ."
We are a real classy bunch.

But Judith had a word for us that first class. Figuratively and literally. She has a PhD from the University of Edinburgh and teaches New Testament and Hermeneutics at Denver Seminary. She told us that knowing the original language of the New Testament was like going from radio to color TV. Understanding the original words and their meaning was a game changer. And she said that it's perplexing to her that an entire theology can be built around one word, especially when it comes to an entire gender. When it comes to God's daughters. And how this one word has been sorely misinterpreted.

Hapax legomenon means "a thing said once"—a term with only one instance of its use recorded. Her example was the word translated as *authority* in 1 Timothy 2:12.

She had our full attention.

The text she referred to comes from Paul's letter to Timothy, who was in Ephesus. Paul was addressing false teachings in his letter and how to handle them. Paul left Timothy in Ephesus to pastor the church there. What was unique about Ephesus was the goddess Artemis of the Ephesians was worshiped there.[1] According to Sandra Glahn, "She (Artemis) is a virgin goddess specializing in several things, including painless delivery or painless deaths, especially related to childbearing."[2] Women in Ephesus, where Timothy was stationed, worshiped the goddess Artemis in hopes that they would not die in childbearing. And this fear isn't a thing of the past. I felt this deeply—even in an age of modern medicine and a much lower mortality rate in childbirth now, I was quite anxious in giving birth to all three of my children and prayed a lot for health, safety, and protection for my baby and myself.

In an interview with Preston Sprinkle on his *Theology in the Raw* podcast, Glahn shared this:

> Artemis in Ephesus both in antiquity . . . and in New Testament times is a goddess of midwifery. She is committed to virginity; she has arrows that can euthanize. I suspect that a woman who is a new Christian who is terrified that the biggest thing she has walked away from as a benefit in Artemis worship is protection in childbirth, which is the number one cause of death for women. And so they are probably praying "either kill me quickly and painlessly or deliver me safely."[3]

Glahn also points to the narrative that Artemis, daughter of Zeus, was born first. She is the firstborn in Greek mythology.

> I no longer think that when [Paul] says Adam was first, that he is giving a principle of male firstness or preeminence. . . . It's a better hermeneutic to see Paul is using a creation story to correct a false creation story and what follows in Adam and Eve's story from the Fall.[4]

When we read Paul's letter to Timothy that says "I do not permit a woman to teach or assume authority over a man," this makes a lot more sense in light of the cult worship of Artemis of Ephesus. Paul is writing to correct false doctrine about Artemis being the one who saves. Paul is saying, *We will trust in God over Artemis.* Cultural context, historical background, and the original language really do bring it all into color TV.

Here's what Paul writes:

> A woman should learn in quietness and full submission. I do not permit a woman to teach or to assume authority over

a man; she must be quiet. For Adam was formed first, then Eve. And Adam was not the one deceived; it was the woman who was deceived and became a sinner. But women will be saved through childbearing—if they continue in faith, love and holiness with propriety.

1 Timothy 2:11–15

First Timothy 2 can be full of hard things to hear for us daughters. We see the words *quietness, full submission, authority, deceived, saved through childbearing*. How does this all work?

As my professor Dr. Judith Diehl pointed out, the word *authentein* in the Greek—translated as *authority*—is only used one time in the entire Bible. This word "indicates absolute control or complete dominance over another individual or over a group."[5] This word is not used anywhere else except right here, in this letter to Timothy, to the church in Ephesus. Per Glahn's research, Paul wanted false doctrines to cease being taught by women who worshiped Artemis. He wanted to quiet this teaching, to have these women learn the truth, and to have them understand that God is the one who saves in every way. This passage seems very tied to women who worshiped Artemis.

Let's keep in mind two things: the entire redemptive narrative we have looked at from the beginning in Genesis to now, and Paul's heart and high regard for women, especially in his glowing statements about all the women and co-laborers in Romans 16.

As a daughter who teaches the Bible, I felt this passage stick its leg out at me often, as if it wanted to trip me up. But perhaps it was simply trying to get my attention so I could move in close, sit with it, and understand it better. I had to sit with Paul's words, I had to do my research, and I had to know if I could teach and operate with whatever authority God has given me in whatever season at whatever time.

As I was reading and listening and exploring these ideas, the redemptive narrative of the story of God was the anchor that kept me teaching, even if I was unsure of a few passages. I went back to the fact that God breathed His breath into humanity, and both men and women equally are made in His image. Women all over the Old and New Testament did all the things: prophesied, led, taught, evangelized, and shepherded. Jesus invited and welcomed and encouraged women to learn from Him and be with Him and to heal with Him and to be sent by Him. And women carried the good news straight from the grave that first resurrection morning, opening their mouths and teaching what was true, just as Phoebe took Paul's letter and taught it in several churches.

And now I see that Paul wanted women to be learners of the gospel of God and not to teach false things. He had a high respect for women who had teaching and leadership roles (like Phoebe and Priscilla, as we looked at in previous chapters). As well, this definition of the onetime use of the word *authentein* is unique to this circumstance. No one—man or woman—should dominate in exercising authority. If fact, one of the most beautiful and paramount descriptions of Jesus is that of a humble servant in Philippians 2. He did not grasp at power, at authority, at a name for Himself. And note Paul's preface to this passage—it is about relating to one another. He says, "In your relationships with one another . . ." (Philippians 2:5). This is what it looks like to interact with one another, to operate in the church, to be brothers and sisters and sons and daughters and aunts and uncles and grandmas and grandpas—to be family—whether we are in positions of power and authority or not:

> In your relationships with one another, have the
> same mindset as Christ Jesus:
> Who, being in very nature God,
> did not consider equality with God something to
> be used to his own advantage;
> rather, he made himself nothing
> by taking the very nature of a servant,
> being made in human likeness.
> And being found in appearance as a man,
> he humbled himself
> by becoming obedient to death—
> even death on a cross!
>
> Therefore God exalted him to the highest place
> and gave him the name that is above every name,
> that at the name of Jesus every knee should bow,
> in heaven and on earth and under the earth,
> and every tongue acknowledge that Jesus Christ is
> Lord,
> to the glory of God the Father.
>
> Philippians 2:5–11

God's vision for a flourishing humanity has always been bigger and fuller and more beautiful than what we often have an imagination for. Even in what is arguably the oldest book of the entire Bible, Job, we see God's heart being woven into the oldest manuscripts. We see a glimpse of the fullness of the redemption of His original design for both men and women, for sons and daughters. Job's story tells us that he had seven sons and three daughters in the beginning of the book. None of them are named. After enduring the loss of his children and the suffering of so much in his story, God gives him back a double portion of what he began with.

> The LORD blessed the latter part of Job's life more than the former part. He had fourteen thousand sheep, six thousand camels, a thousand yoke of oxen and a thousand donkeys. And he also had seven sons and three daughters. The first daughter he named Jemimah, the second Keziah and the third Keren-Happuch. Nowhere in all the land were there found women as beautiful as Job's daughters, and their father granted them an inheritance along with their brothers. After this, Job lived a hundred and forty years; he saw his children and their children to the fourth generation. And so Job died, an old man and full of years.
>
> Job 42:12–17

Don't miss these two details: Job's daughters are named, and Job's daughters are given an inheritance. These two stunning facts are significant in this cultural context (there is only one other place in the Bible where women are given an inheritance, in Numbers 27:1–4). It seems Job experienced great suffering; encountered a generous, redemptive, and compassionate God; and in turn, became a generous, redemptive, and compassionate father. Judy Allen shares this about the notes on Job 42:10–17 in *Matthew Henry's Commentary*:

> Matthew Henry alone notes that [his daughters] could have been named to reflect Job's experience: Jemima meant the day, which was a nice change from the dark night, Kezia, was a fragrant smelling spice, and Keren-happuch meant plenty restored, and Henry says "perhaps they excelled their brethren in wisdom and piety."[6]

The daughters of Job give us an anchoring hope in our ancient collective history. Daughters are seen, named, blessed, and given co-ruling responsibilities. We have a rich inheritance from our Father.

As you receive your daughtership, I'd like to shower you with blessings and reminders about who you are.

Daughters Are Ambassadors

Paul writes in his letter to the Corinthians, "We are therefore Christ's ambassadors, as though God were making his appeal through us" (2 Corinthians 5:20). The word *ambassadors* in this verse comes from the Greek word *presbeúō*, which "means to act as an established statesman (diplomat)—a trusted, respected ambassador who is authorized to speak as God's emissary (represent His kingdom)."[7] We are authorized—endowed with authority—to be God's ambassadors, sons and daughters alike, with the ministry of reconciliation as our message.

Daughters Are Royalty

Peter writes,

> But you are a chosen people, a royal priesthood, a holy nation, God's special possession, that you may declare the praises of him who called you out of darkness into his wonderful light. Once you were not a people, but now you are the people of God; once you had not received mercy, but now you have received mercy.
>
> 1 Peter 2:9–10

Daughters are part of the royal priesthood. Our crown can never be taken from us, and our royal status cannot be removed. We belong to God as his princesses. We are His.

Daughters Are Co-Heirs

Paul writes,

> For those who are led by the Spirit of God are the children of God. The Spirit you received does not make you slaves, so that you live in fear again; rather, the Spirit you received brought about your adoption to sonship. And by him we cry, *"Abba, Father."* The Spirit himself testifies with our spirit that we are God's children. Now if we are children, then we are heirs—heirs of God and co-heirs with Christ, if indeed we share in his sufferings in order that we may also share in his glory.
>
> Romans 8:14–17

We are co-heirs. Whatever inheritance Jesus has, He shares with us.

Daughters Are Powerful

Paul writes, "And if the Spirit of him who raised Jesus from the dead is living in you, he who raised Christ from the dead will also give life to your mortal bodies because of his Spirit who lives in you" (Romans 8:11). Later he says the same thing to the Ephesians: The same power that rose Christ from the dead lives in you through the Spirit. Daughters are full of power from the Spirit of God.

Daughters Are Commissioned

Jesus commissions His followers to go—in His name and because of His authority—to make disciples, baptize, and teach. It's the Great Commission, the great call, to any and all followers, sons and daughters alike. It is the touchstone and the mission of the church, and it is for all of us.

And so it feels fitting and right, in this last section of receiving our name as daughters, to also remind you that you are sent in His powerful and authoritative name to make disciples, to baptize, and to teach everything God has commanded us. And surely, He is with us. He is in us. We belong to Him, we find healing in Him, and we receive this commission from Him:

> Then Jesus came to them and said, "All authority in heaven and on earth has been given to me. Therefore go and make disciples of all nations, baptizing them in the name of the Father and of the Son and of the Holy Spirit, and teaching them to obey everything I have commanded you. And surely I am with you always, to the very end of the age.
>
> Matthew 28:18–20

Your name is daughter, and the Father created you in His image. He gives breath to your body, and He has called you and empowered you and commissioned you, pouring out His life-giving Spirit upon you and giving you gifts to edify and build up the body of believers. You can see the landscape of the daughters who have gone before you, and you can draw great strength from their good, hard works—their fiery spirits in battle, their pouring out of their heart in God's house, their healed hearts and bold messianic claims, their commission from Jesus that first Easter morning.

There's nothing you cannot do if your Father calls you to it. You can walk into any room with your head held high, confident, beautiful, using your voice to speak life, your gifts to build up others, your hands to hold the hurting, your heart to hold the grace to keep going when it all feels uncertain. And you can be certain of this: The unsung women who have gone before you show you that God's daughters are beloved, are wanted, and are needed in every space in the kingdom of God.

So if you would be so bold, dear daughter, wherever you find yourself reading this, may you open your hands and your heart to receive this priestly blessing that I bless you with from our powerful God:

> The LORD bless you
>   and keep you;
> The LORD make his face shine on you
>   and be gracious to you;
> the LORD turn his face toward you
>   and give you peace.
>
> Numbers 6:24–26

ACKNOWLEDGMENTS

To my love, Rob Seiffert. You have heard my questions, my discoveries, my tears, my heart about women for years. And you held space for it all. You have been an unbelievable support, reading what I am reading, asking questions along with me. There is no way I could have written this book without you. You make sure I know my name.

To my kids, Robby, Olive, Judah. You are always telling me to do it. To do seminary. To write the book. To speak at the gig. To fly to the place. To give it a go. You are my heart. I love you guys. Remember Whose you are. You are sons and daughters of the Most High King. Talk it all over with your Heavenly Father first.

To Jamie, Sara, Erin. And to Marco Polo, which has hosted our tales for several years. You guys have held so much space for me, and I adore you so. May we find Mexican restaurants and wear matching pj's at least once a year.

To Trinity and Lindsay. You guys hear my whispers, my questions, my discoveries. Thank you for being such gifts.

To Jami Nato. Thank you for being an instant friend, a kind soul, a hilarious companion in seminary. You said,

"Me, too" a million times, and I couldn't believe I have such a gift of encouragement in you. You are Barnabas. God was having fun when He designed our cohort.

To Dr. Don Payne. I wasn't expecting such a pastoral academic dean and professor of theology. Thank you for holding space for our questions, tears, and experiences as you blew our minds and prayed for us, over and over. You gained sixteen seminary daughters, and we are not sorry.

To my seminary sisters. You GUYS. We are being formed in every possible way by one another. Through prayer, tears, laughter, lament, fear, anxiety, and hope, we are doing this. We, like Mary, are at Jesus's feet, crossing all kinds of boundaries to learn like one of His disciples. Thank you for letting me share deep things and for loving me so well and for contributing to this book either with your actual words or your prayers or your love.

To JDL. You are an absolute queen at this, and I am beyond grateful you wanted to do this together. Thank you for pushing me, helping me, hearing me, encouraging me. This is not a book if it wasn't for you.

To the Soma City staff team. Y'all know how to use confetti. The generosity in your hearts with your love, joy, thoughtfulness, coaching, wisdom, notes, and cheering is next level. Thank you for welcoming me. I adore you each. Boom boom!

RESOURCES

There have been many resources that were immensely forma-
tive for this book and in my life. I want to highlight some
of them here for further study of works by scholars who
have studied much deeper than I have and who help us to
understand passages that talk about submission, women as
leaders, teachers, elders, living as emboldened women in
ministry, vindicating women in the Bible who have been given
a bad rap, and more. My hope and prayer with this book is to
bring women to life in new fresh ways, to see some narratives
from a different angle, and to allow God's face to shine upon
us, as women, when perhaps it has felt shadowy and dark.

The Blue Parakeet: Rethinking How You Read the Bible
by Scot McKnight
*Emboldened: A Vision for Empowering Women in Min-
istry* by Tara Beth Leach
*The Making of Biblical Womanhood: How the Subju-
gation of Women Became Gospel Truth* by Beth Allison Barr

Tell Her Story: How Women Led, Taught, and Ministered in the Early Church by Nijay K. Gupta

Nobody's Mother: Artemis of the Ephesians in Antiquity and the New Testament by Sandra L. Glahn

Vindicating the Vixens: Revisiting Sexualized, Vilified, and Marginalized Women of the Bible edited by Sandra Glahn

The Real Mary: Why Evangelical Christians Can Embrace the Mother of Jesus by Scot McKnight

Holy Curiosity, a podcast by Kat Armstrong

A podcast series on "Defining a Biblical Position on Women and Eldership" from Bridgetown Church in Portland, Oregon:

Tyler Staton, "Lecture: Part 1: Women & Eldership—What Is Our Position?"

https://www.youtube.com/watch?v=PKetqpnVI24

Tyler Staton, "Lecture: Part 2: Women & Eldership—What Does This Mean for Me?"

https://www.youtube.com/watch?v=08RcatbWyxE

Tyler Staton, "Lecture: Part 3: Women & Eldership—A Closer Look at the Four Pillars"

https://www.youtube.com/watch?v=x-VGy7Q4aYk

Tyler Staton, Bethany Allen, and Gavin Bennett, "Lecture: Part 4: Women & Eldership—Threats and Invitations"

https://www.youtube.com/watch?v=bU5jMdSIPxg

NOTES

Introduction

1. Tara Beth Leach, "Women in Ministry | Tara Beth Leach | Seminary Now Scene," Seminary Now, March 7, 2024, YouTube video, 1:07, https://www.youtube.com/watch?v=bzjRBIzcUFI.

Chapter 1 The Daughter: We Are Named

1. Richard Bauckham, *Gospel Women: Studies of the Named Women in the Gospels* (Grand Rapids, MI: W. B. Eerdmans, 2002), 112.

2. This concept of the backdrop but not the blueprint of the Bible being patriarchy comes from Carolyn Custis James. See her book *Finding God in the Margins* and article "Dismantling Patriarchy to Recover the Blessed Alliance (Part 2)," May 23, 2024, Awakenings 2023 Gathering plenary keynote lecture, https://www.missioalliance.org/dismantling-patriarchy-to-recover-the-blessed-alliance-part-2/.

3. N. T. Wright, *Jesus and the Victory of God: Christian Origins and the Question of God*, vol. 2 (Minneapolis: Fortress Press, 1996), 278.

4. "Meaning of Numbers: The Number 12," BibleStudy.org, accessed February 15, 2023, https://www.biblestudy.org/bibleref/meaning-of-numbers-in-bible/12.html.

5. Shuvangi B, "Neelkarunji—the Flowers That Blossom Once in 12 Years," TimesOfIndia.com, January 13, 2024, https://timesofindia.indiatimes.com/etimes/trending/the-season-of-neelakarunji-flowers-that-bloom-once-in-12-years-is-back/photostory/106808933.cms?picid=106808944.

6. James R. Edwards, *The Gospel According to Luke: The Pillar New Testament Commentary* (Grand Rapids, MI: W. B. Eerdmans, 2015), 257.

Chapter 2 The Ezer: We Have Always Belonged

1. Chaim Bentorah, "Hebrew Word Study—Love—Tov Mo'ed— טוב מאד," January 2021, Biblical Hebrew Studies, https://www.chaimbento rah.com/2021/01/hebrew-word-study-love-tov-moed-טוב-מאד/.

2. Margaret Mowczko, "The Holy Spirit and Eve as Helpers," August 1, 2019, https://margmowczko.com/holy-spirit-eve-helpers/.

3. Tim Mackie and Jon Collins, "Why Cain Builds a City," BibleProject podcast *The City*, episode 2, May 1, 2023, 1:30, https://bibleproject.com /podcast/why-cain-builds-city/.

4. Shara Drimalla and the BibleProject Team, "3 Love Stories in the Bible That Help Us Rethink Romance," BibleProject, February 8, 2023, https://bibleproject.com/articles/romantic-relationships-in-the-bible/.

5. Tim Mackie and Jon Collins, "Why Cain Builds a City," BibleProject podcast *The City*, episode 2, May 1, 2023, 1:30, https://bibleproject.com /podcast/why-cain-builds-city/.

6. Glenn Kreider, "Chapter 6: Eve: The Mother of All Seducers?" in *Vindicating the Vixens: Revisiting Sexualized, Vilified, and Marginalized Women of the Bible*, ed. Sandra Glahn (Grand Rapids, MI: Kregel Academic, 2017), 136.

7. Scot McKnight, *The Blue Parakeet: Rethinking How You Read the Bible,* 2nd ed. (Grand Rapids, MI: Zondervan, 2018), 240.

8. Preston M. Sprinkle, *Embodied: Transgender Identities, the Church, and What the Bible Has to Say* (Colorado Springs, CO: David C. Cook, 2021), 68.

9. Shara Drimalla and the BibleProject Team, "3 Love Stories in the Bible That Help Us Rethink Romance," BibleProject, February 8, 2023, https://bibleproject.com/articles/romantic-relationships-in-the-bible/.

Chapter 4 The Womb: We Have Bodies That Belong

1. Jon Collins, Tim Mackie, and Carissa Quinn, "The Womb of God?" BibleProject podcast *Character of God*, episode 3, August 31, 2020, 0:58, https://bibleproject.com/podcast/the-womb-of-god/.

2. Jess Connolly, *Breaking Free from Body Shame* (Grand Rapids, MI: Zondervan, 2021), 32.

3. Jon Collins, Tim Mackie, and Carissa Quinn, "The Womb of God?" BibleProject podcast *Character of God*, episode 3, August 31, 2020,19:06–19:25, 30:55, 1:55, https://bibleproject.com/podcast/the-womb-of-god/.

4. Shiao Chong, "Biblical Maternal Images for God," The Junia Project, May 7, 2016, https://juniaproject.com/biblical-maternal-images-for-god/.

5. Jon Collins, Tim Mackie, and Carissa Quinn, "The Womb of God?" BibleProject podcast show notes, https://bibleproject.com/podcast/the -womb-of-god/.

Chapter 5 The Prophet: We Have Voices That Belong

1. Scot McKnight, *The Blue Parakeet: Rethinking How You Read Your Bible* (Grand Rapids, MI: Zondervan, 2018), 225.

2. "Typically, the person of lower status or honor would be summoned to the presence of the person with higher honor." Christa L. McKirland, "Chapter 10: Huldah: Malfunction with the Wardrobe-Keeper's Wife," in *Vindicating the Vixens: Revisiting Sexualized, Vilified, and Marginalized Women of the Bible*, ed. Sandra Glahn (Grand Rapids, MI: Kregel Academic, 2017), 221.

3. Cassandra Gill, "11 Things about Women in Ancient Israel You Probably Didn't Know," OUPblog, October 27, 2016, https://blog.oup.com/2016/10/women-ancient-israel/.

4. Christa McKirland tells us, "Likely, her husband managed the wardrobe of the priests, since he was of the Levitical line." Christa L. Mc Kirland, "Chapter 10: Huldah: Malfunction with the Wardrobe-Keeper's Wife," in *Vindicating the Vixens: Revisiting Sexualized, Vilified, and Marginalized Women of the Bible*, ed. Sandra Glahn (Grand Rapids, MI: Kregel Academic, 2017), 221.

5. Christa L. McKirland, "Chapter 10: Huldah: Malfunction with the Wardrobe-Keeper's Wife," in *Vindicating the Vixens: Revisiting Sexualized, Vilified, and Marginalized Women of the Bible*, ed. Sandra Glahn (Grand Rapids, MI: Kregel Academic, 2017), 223.

6. Christa L. McKirland, "Chapter 10: Huldah: Malfunction with the Wardrobe-Keeper's Wife," in *Vindicating the Vixens: Revisiting Sexualized, Vilified, and Marginalized Women of the Bible*, ed. Sandra Glahn (Grand Rapids, MI: Kregel Academic, 2017), 222.

7. Scot McKnight, *The Blue Parakeet: Rethinking How You Read Your Bible* (Grand Rapids, MI: Zondervan, 2018), 225.

8. Rev. Olga and Rev. Stephen Shaffer, "Huldah: Bold Prophetess of God," in *She Is Called: Women of the Bible Study Series Vol. 3*, accessed August 25, 2023, https://www.faithward.org/women-of-the-bible-study-series/huldah-bold-prophetess-of-god/.

Chapter 7 The Heroes: We Belong with Our Leadership

1. "Typically, the person of lower status or honor would be summoned to the presence of the person with higher honor." Christa L. McKirland, "Chapter 10: Huldah: Malfunction with the Wardrobe-Keeper's Wife," in *Vindicating the Vixens: Revisiting Sexualized, Vilified, and Marginalized Women of the Bible*, ed. Sandra Glahn (Grand Rapids, MI: Kregel Academic, 2017), 221.

2. Scot McKnight, *The Blue Parakeet: Rethinking How You Read Your Bible* (Grand Rapids, MI: Zondervan, 2018), 220.

3. Ron Pierce writes, "Barak is mentioned only twice in Scriptures: 1 Samuel 12:9–11 and Hebrews 11:32–28. . . . Both of these references to Barak portray him in a positive light as a courageous warrior and person of faith (i.e. 'a worthy man')." Ron Pierce, "Chapter 9: Deborah: Only When a Good Man Is Hard to Find?" in *Vindicating the Vixens: Revisiting Sexualized, Vilified, and Marginalized Women of the Bible*, ed. Sandra Glahn (Grand Rapids, MI: Kregel Academic, 2017), 196–97.

4. Ron Pierce writes, "By the time of Deborah, Jael's group had separated itself from the rest of the other Kenites and migrated (literally, 'pitched their tents') to Naphtali territory, where her family had allied with King Jabin to live under his protection (4:11, 17)." Ron Pierce, "Chapter 9: Deborah: Only When a Good Man Is Hard to Find?" in *Vindicating the Vixens: Revisiting Sexualized, Vilified, and Marginalized Women of the Bible*, ed. Sandra Glahn (Grand Rapids, MI: Kregel Academic, 2017), 200.

5. "Jael," Women in the Bible, WomenInScripture.com, accessed August 31, 2023, https://womeninscripture.com/jael/.

Chapter 8 The Immigrant: We Are Fully Welcomed

1. *Why?* we might ask. According to *The Lexham Bible Dictionary*,
The reason given for their banishment from the assembly is twofold:
1. They did not provide the Israelites with food and water when they were journeying out of Egypt.
2. They hired Balaam to curse the Israelites (Num 22–24).
Kim Williams Bodenhamer, "Ruth, Book of," in *The Lexham Bible Dictionary*, ed. John D. Barry (Bellingham, WA: Lexham Press, 2012).

2. Kim Williams Bodenhamer, "Ruth, Book of," in *The Lexham Bible Dictionary*, ed. John D. Barry (Bellingham, WA: Lexham Press, 2012).

3. Charlie Garrett, "Ruth 3:14–18 (Shesh Seorim – Six Measures of Barley," sermon, October 5, 2014, The Superior Word, https://superiorword.org/ruth-3-14-18-shesh-seorim-six-measures-of-barley/.

Chapter 9 The Forgotten: We Are Remembered

1. "What Does the Bible Mean When It Says That God Remembered Something?" GotQuestions.org, accessed September 11, 2023, https://www.gotquestions.org/God-remembered.html.

Chapter 10 The Nameless: We Are Important

1. David Guzik, "2 Kings 5—Naaman the Leper," *Enduring Word Commentary*, 2018, https://enduringword.com/bible-commentary/2-kings-5/.

2. David Guzik, "2 Kings 5—Naaman the Leper," *Enduring Word Commentary*, 2018, https://enduringword.com/bible-commentary/2-kings-5/.

3. David Guzik, "2 Kings 5—Naaman the Leper," *Enduring Word Commentary*, 2018, https://enduringword.com/bible-commentary/2-kings-5/.

4. James Bryan Smith, *The Good and Beautiful Life* (Downers Grove, IL: IVP, 2009), 55.

Chapter 11 The Marginalized: We Are Valuable

1. Scot McKnight, *The Real Mary* (Brewster, MA: Paraclete Press, 2007), 8.

2. Scot McKnight, *The Real Mary* (Brewster, MA: Paraclete Press, 2007), 18: "In the 1980s the government of Guatemala banned any public reciting of Mary's Magnificat because it was deemed politically subversive."

3. John 2:4 footnote, *New International Version*, BibleGateway, https://www.biblegateway.com/passage/?search=John+2%3A4&version=NIV.

4. Susannah Heschel, quoting her father in her introduction to *Moral Grandeur and Spiritual Audacity: Essays*, by Abraham Joshua Heschel, ed. by Susannah Heschel (New York: Farrar, Straus and Giroux, 1996), viii.

Chapter 12 The Sisterhood: We Were Created for Community

1. *Merriam-Webster Unabridged Dictionary*, s.v. "proximity," accessed July 25, 2024, https://unabridged.merriam-webster.com/unabridged/proximity.

Chapter 13 The Condemned: We Are Covered by His Love

1. N. T. Wright, "#71 Should the Story of the Woman Caught in Adultery Be in Our Bible?" June 24, 2021, *Ask NT Wright Anything* podcast, 7:49, https://open.spotify.com/episode/7xwAGZpo2QrW0sSSAAR9Ai.

2. Bryan Crum, *Neighbor, Love Yourself: Discover Your Value, Live Your Worth* (Colorado Springs, CO: WaterBrook, 2024), 120.

3. N. T. Wright, "Those Whom He Justified, He Also Glorified," February 22, 2013, https://ntwrightpage.com/2016/03/30/those-whom-he-justified-he-also-glorified/.

Chapter 14 The Disciple Sisters: We Are Disciples

1. N. T. Wright, "Women's Service in the Church: The Biblical Basis," September 4, 2004, https://ntwrightpage.com/2016/07/12/womens-service-in-the-church-the-biblical-basis/.

2. Lucy Peppiatt, "Misunderstanding Mary and Martha," August 31, 2023, https://www.premierchristianity.com/columnists/misunderstanding-mary-and-martha/16186.article.

3. Richard Bauckman, *Jesus and the Eyewitnesses: The Gospels as Eyewitness Testimony*, 2nd ed. (Grand Rapids, MI: W. B. Eerdmans, 2017), 130.

Chapter 15 The First: We Are Called Upon

1. Lynn Cohick, "Chapter 12: The 'Woman at the Well': Was the Samaritan Woman Really an Adulteress?" in *Vindicating the Vixens: Revisiting Sexualized, Vilified, and Marginalized Women of the Bible*, ed. Sandra Glahn (Grand Rapids, MI: Kregel Academic, 2017), 251.

2. Lynn Cohick, "Chapter 12: The 'Woman at the Well': Was the Samaritan Woman Really an Adulteress?" in *Vindicating the Vixens: Revisiting Sexualized, Vilified, and Marginalized Women of the Bible*, ed. Sandra Glahn (Grand Rapids, MI: Kregel Academic, 2017), 251.

3. Darlene M. Seal, "NT501 Class Lecture," (lecture, Denver Seminary, January 23, 2024).

4. I learned about this idea from the podcast *Holy Curiosity*, which over a series of episodes unpacks many of the ideas in Kat Armstrong's book *The In-Between Place*. See Kat Armstrong, *The In-Between Place: Where Jesus Changes Your Story* (Nashville: W Publishing, 2021) and *Holy Curiosity* podcast by Kat Armstrong, https://www.christianitytoday.com/ct/podcasts/holy-curiosity/.

Chapter 16 The Fellow Workers: We Are Honored

1. Nijay K. Gupta, *Tell Her Story: How Women Led, Taught, and Ministered in the Early Church* (Downers Grove, IL: IVP Academic, 2023), 119.

2. Scot McKnight, *The Blue Parakeet: Rethinking How You Read Your Bible* (Grand Rapids, MI: Zondervan, 2018), 235.

3. Beth Allison Barr, "I Knew the Truth About Women in the Bible and I Stayed Silent," Baptist News Global, April 7, 2021, https://baptistnews.com/article/i-knew-the-truth-about-women-in-the-bible-and-i-stayed-silent/.

4. Beth Allison Barr, "I Knew the Truth About Women in the Bible and I Stayed Silent," Baptist News Global, April 7, 2021, https://baptistnews.com/article/i-knew-the-truth-about-women-in-the-bible-and-i-stayed-silent/.

5. Bronwen Speedie, "Who's Who in Paul's Greetings in Romans 16 (Part 1)," God's Design—Perth, January 16, 2019, https://godsdesignperth.org/2019/01/16/whos-who-in-pauls-greetings-in-romans-16-part-1/.

6. Megan Briggs, "N. T. Wright: The New Testament is Clear on Female Preachers," February 21, 2020, https://churchleaders.com/news/371359

-what-does-the-bible-say-about-female-preachers.html?fbclid=IwAR3E
c2xgJrpueSJfT2e2F4MrqDhOPqclaP2g16N0kHbiERiaBETURMIYXL0.

7. Scot McKnight, *The Blue Parakeet: Rethinking How You Read Your Bible* (Grand Rapids, MI: Zondervan, 2018), 235.

8. Nijay K. Gupta, *Tell Her Story: How Women Led, Taught, and Ministered in the Early Church* (Downers Grove, IL: IVP Academic, 2023), 126.

9. Lisa Bowens, "African American Readings of Paul with Dr. Lisa Bowens—KR 203," October 6, 2022, interview by Scot McKnight, *Kingdom Roots with Scot McKnight* podcast, 18:50–19:39, https://podfollow.com /1078739516/episode/7f5d0a52c83a707cb97a4fe242e69f303dae9f34/view.

10. Michael F. Bird, *Romans: The Story of God Bible Commentary*, vol. 6 (Grand Rapids, MI: Zondervan, 2016), 522–23.

11. Lynn H. Cohick, "Priscilla and Aquilla," Bible Odyssey, accessed January 9, 2024, https://blog.bibleodyssey.org/articles/priscilla-and-aquila/.

12. Nijay K. Gupta, *Tell Her Story: How Women Led, Taught, and Ministered in the Early Church* (Downers Grove, IL: IVP Academic, 2023), 51.

Chapter 17 The Single Women: We Are Family

1. Tara-Leigh Cobble, "Episode 227: The Gift of Singleness (feat. Tara-Leigh Cobble)," *Becoming Something with Jonathan Pokluda* podcast, August 14, 2023, 10:00, https://www.youtube.com/watch?v=HQ0Fka-VDWo.

2. A. J. Swoboda and Nijay K. Gupta, "Episode 26: A Spirituality of Singleness," *Slow Theology* podcast, September 2023, 12:46, https://open .spotify.com/episode/7bNTNbNMeODY74pL0fTg1m.

3. Carolyn Custis James, "Chapter 1: Tamar: The Righteous Prostitute," in *Vindicating the Vixens: Revisiting Sexualized, Vilified, and Marginalized Women of the Bible*, ed. Sandra Glahn (Grand Rapids, MI: Kregel Academic, 2017), 45.

4. A. J. Swoboda and Nijay K. Gupta, "Episode 26: A Spirituality of Singleness," *Slow Theology* podcast, September 2023, 1:15, https://open .spotify.com/episode/7bNTNbNMeODY74pL0fTg1m.

5. A. J. Swoboda and Nijay K. Gupta, "Episode 26: A Spirituality of Singleness," *Slow Theology* podcast, September 2023, 22:49, https://open .spotify.com/episode/7bNTNbNMeODY74pL0fTg1m.

Chapter 18 The Grandmas: We Are Needed

1. Blair Parke, "What Do We Know about Timothy in the Bible?" May 25, 2022, Bible Study Tools, https://www.biblestudytools.com/bible-study /topical-studies/what-do-we-know-about-timothy-in-the-bible.html.

Chapter 19 The Spirit-Filled Daughters: We Are Filled with God

1. I highly recommend Propel Cohorts: https://cohorts.propelwomen .org/.

2. "Who was Anna in the Bible?" January 10, 2023, Basilica of the National Shrine of the Immaculate Conception, https://www.national shrine.org/blog/who-was-anna-in-the-bible/.

3. Emily Hall, "Who was Anna in the Bible?" July 12, 2019, Christianity.com, https://www.christianity.com/wiki/people/who-was-anna -in-the-bible.html.

4. Beth Allison Barr, *The Making of Biblical Womanhood* (Grand Rapids, MI: Brazos Press, 2021), 147–8.

5. Tara Beth Leach (@tarabeth82), "Let's Talk Women in Ministry: 5 Reminders for Women in Ministry," January 30, 2024, Instagram photo, https:// www.instagram.com/p/C2vc1qWPiWf/?igsh=dmMzdWg3b3AzOGl3.

Chapter 20 The Daughters of Job: We Have an Inheritance

1. Chesna Hinkley, "What to Say When Someone Says Women Are Not Permitted to Teach," February 14, 2019, CBE International, https://www .cbeinternational.org/resource/what-say-when-someone-says-women-are -not-permitted-teach/.

2. Sandra Glahn, *Nobody's Mother: Artemis of the Ephesians in Antiquity and the New Testament* (Downers Grove, IL: IVP, 2023), chapter 3, 23:37, Audible.

3. Sandra Glahn, "Artemis, Ephesus, and the Background to 1 Timothy 2: Dr. Sandra Glahn," March 20, 2023, *Theology in the Raw* podcast, 17:20, https://www.youtube.com/watch?v=xoxzQkAy8u8.

4. Sandra Glahn, "Artemis, Ephesus, and the Background to 1 Timothy 2: Dr. Sandra Glahn," March 20, 2023, *Theology in the Raw* podcast, 1:09:27, https://www.youtube.com/watch?v=xoxzQkAy8u8.

5. Randall Merrill, 2014, "Authority," in *The Lexham Theological Wordbook*, s.v. *"authentein,"* ed. Douglas Mangum, et. al. (Bellingham, WA: Lexham Press, 2014), Logos Bible software.

6. Judy Allen, "Inheritance for Everyone," May 17, 2018, Connecting DotsToGod.com, https://connectingdotstogod.com/2018/05/17/inheri tance-for-everyone/.

7. HELPS Word-studies, s.v. "4243. presbeuó," Bible Hub, accessed January 31, 2024, https://biblehub.com/greek/4243.htm.

AMY SEIFFERT is an author, speaker, pastor, and YouVersion Bible teacher. She serves on the teaching team at her home church, Soma City, and is currently attending Denver Seminary for a master's in biblical and theological studies. Through her speaking and writing, Amy uses humor, storytelling, and biblical teaching to invite women to discover grace in their daily lives. She loves playing tennis and eating moose tracks ice cream, preferably in that order. Amy is married to Rob, and they live in Bowling Green, Ohio, with their three kids.

CONNECT WITH AMY:

AmySeiffert.com

 @AmySeiffertBlog

 @AmySeiffert

 @AmySeiffert1